MIND
MANAGEMENT
NOT
TIME
MANAGEMENT

ALSO BY DAVID KADAVY

The Heart to Start: Stop Procrastinating & Start Creating

Design for Hackers: Reverse-Engineering Beauty

MIND
MANAGEMENT
NOT
TIME
MANAGEMENT

Productivity When Creativity Matters

DAVID KADAVY

KADAVY INC.

TABLE OF CONTENTS

1 MIND MANAGEMENT, NOT TIME MANAGEMENT   9

WELCOME TO THE CREATIVE AGE. 15

THE END OF TIME MANAGEMENT 19

TIME WORSHIP. 23

WHEN YOU SAVE TIME, KEEP IT. 26

THE TWO FALSE ASSUMPTIONS OF TIME MANAGEMENT 28

BEYOND TIME MANAGEMENT. 31

WHY I MOVED TO ANOTHER CONTINENT. 34

FROM A TIME MANAGEMENT WORLD
TO A MIND MANAGEMENT WORLD 37

2 CREATIVE SWEET SPOT   41

DIVERGENT/CONVERGENT 44

A MICROCOSM OF CREATIVITY. 46

THE SUDDEN NATURE OF INSIGHT 49

ILLUMINATING THE NOT-SO-OBVIOUS .51

NOT ALL HOURS ARE EQUAL 54

FIRE THE CEO (OF YOUR BRAIN) 57

CREATE THE CONDITIONS FOR COLLISION 59

THE FIRST-HOUR RULE. 61

THE GIFT OF GROGGY. 63

FLIPPING THE TEMPORAL SWITCH 66

WHY ARE THERE EIGHT DAYS IN A WEEK? 68

CREATIVITY IS A MAZE, NOT A JOGGING PATH 70

THE HIGH INTEREST RATE OF BORROWED TIME 74

MAKING UP TIME. 76

QUADRUPLING MY CREATIVE OUTPUT .79

3 THE FOUR STAGES OF CREATIVITY   83

IDEAS NEVER COME TO A WEARIED BRAIN 85

FROM THE INSIDE OUT. 89

CREATIVITY IS SHORT-TERM MEMORY MANAGEMENT 91

MICHELANGELO WAS NO GOD 94

THE FOUR STAGES OF YESTERDAY 97

HOW INCUBATION WORKS 99

RESPECT THE FOUR STAGES. 102

4 THE SEVEN MENTAL STATES OF CREATIVE WORK   105

THE SEVEN MENTAL STATES. 109

FLAVORS OF DEEP WORK 112

FUZZY BORDERS 114

STAY IN STATE 119

TOOLS FOR THOUGHT: THE SLIPPY & THE GRIPPY 122

MAKE THE ROOM WORK FOR YOU 126

YOUR OWN PERSONAL PLACEBO 130

5 CREATIVE CYCLES   135

COASTING WITH CYCLES 138

QUIT YOUR DAILY ROUTINE. START YOUR WEEKLY ROUTINE. . . . 140

WHAT I LEARNED ABOUT PRODUCTIVITY
WHILE WORKING ON GOOGLE CALENDAR 146

MENTAL STATES THROUGHOUT THE WEEK 150

THE POWERFUL RULE 155

PREFRONTAL MONDAY 156

PRIORITIZE PRIORITIZATION WITH THE WEEKLY REVIEW 158

EMPLOY YOUR PASSIVE GENIUS. 163

WHEN THERE'S ONLY "NOW," YOU WON'T PROCRASTINATE 166

WEEK OF WANT 167

CYCLES IN CULTURAL CUES. 170

6 CREATIVE SYSTEMS   175

MORE THAN ONE CUPCAKE 181

MINIMUM CREATIVE DOSE. 183

CYCLES IN SYSTEMS 188

SOP: SLOPPY OPERATING PROCEDURE 191

THE POWERFUL POWER OF REPETITION 194

FRONT BURNER/BACK BURNER 198

CREATIVE CONSTRAINTS 201

FLY HIGH WITH PILOTS. 204

WHY AM I CHANGING MY CLOTHES
IN A FILTHY LAUNDROMAT BATHROOM? 207

7 CREATING IN CHAOS   211

HOW TO KEEP GOING WHEN YOUR LIFE IS A DUMPSTER FIRE. . . . 217

ORGANIZE BY MENTAL STATE 220

DO WHAT YOU CAN WITH WHAT YOU HAVE 223

CREATIVE OPPORTUNITIES 225

THE CREATIVE CASCADE 229

TASK TRIGGERS 231

CREATIVE SIMMER 237

NOTHING HAPPENS FOR A REASON, BUT IT DOES HAPPEN 239

EPILOGUE   243

ACKNOWLEDGEMENTS   248

NOTES   251

ABOUT THE AUTHOR   260

BONUS MATERIAL

I'VE WRITTEN this book to last for years, but technology moves quickly. If you want to know which tools I currently use to make the most of my creative energy, sign up for my newsletter at kdv.co/tools

CHAPTER 1

MIND MANAGEMENT, NOT TIME MANAGEMENT

Things are not difficult to make;
what is difficult is putting ourselves in
the state of mind to make them.

—CONSTANTIN BRANCUSI

"THERE'S ONLY twenty-four hours in a day." The conclusion we're supposed to draw from this common observation is: If there are only so many hours in a day, you should make the most of each of those precious hours. Time management, it seems, is critically important.

When you start managing your time, you find you really are getting more done. You're keeping a calendar, so you don't forget things. You're building routines, so you can get repeating tasks done faster. You're learning keyboard shortcuts for the apps you use every day. You may even start saying "no" to some opportunities, so you can make better use of your time.

But it becomes harder and harder to get more out of your time. Your calendar becomes jam-packed with a kaleidoscope of colored blocks. You start "speed reading," and listening to audiobooks and podcasts on 3x speed. You start cutting out all but the most essential activities that move you toward your goals. No more lunches with your friends – you'll eat at your desk.

Next, you figure, you can get more out of your time if you do two things at once. So you start multitasking. You're checking your email while brushing your teeth. You're holding conference calls while driving to work.

You start searching for extra bits of time, like loose change under couch cushions. You used to sleep eight hours, but now you'll sleep five. You can check emails at family dinners. You can steal extra hours of work on your laptop after everyone in the house has gone to bed.

You're tired all the time. There's not enough coffee in the world to keep you going. Your anxiety levels are sky-high, and you're becoming forgetful. You're always in a rush.

With each new tactic you learn, each new "life hack," each new shortcut, life gets more hectic. You would start outsourcing some of the load, but you're so busy and so exhausted, you can't even explain what's keeping you so busy. The harder you try to get more out of your time, the less time you have. Even if you did have the time, you wouldn't have the energy.

Until one day you realize: *"There's only twenty-four hours in a day." Maybe that doesn't mean what I thought it meant?*

I thought it meant I should get the most done in the least amount of time possible.

What I'm learning is, if there's only twenty-four hours in a day, that means there's a limit.

I can only get so much out of my time. "Time management" is like squeezing blood from a stone.

THIS STORY is not too different from my own. For my

entire adult life, I have been a productivity enthusiast, with time management as one of my key strategies for getting more done. It started in college. As a graphic design student, I learned all the keyboard shortcuts for Photoshop. I used training software to learn to type faster. When I graduated and got a job, I constantly experimented with different ways of keeping a to-do list and prioritizing my tasks. I pontificated with any colleague who would listen about how to cut down on the number of emails in my inbox. One thing I loved about working in Silicon Valley was that there was no shortage of tech geeks with whom I could swap tips on the latest productivity apps.

Eventually, I ran out of ways to get more done in less time, and my quest went on a detour. That led me to embark on the adventure I'm sharing in this book.

FOUR YEARS ago, I found myself sitting on the bare hardwood floor of my apartment in Chicago, eating lunch from a takeout container with a plastic fork. I had no furniture, no plates, no silverware. I had sold my last chair to some guy from Craigslist fifteen minutes prior.

I was about to embark on my most audacious productivity experiment yet. As I looked around at the three suitcases which housed my final remaining possessions, and the painters erasing from the walls any trace that I had lived there for seven years, I was trying to wrap my head around one fact: That night, I would fall asleep in another country. For the foreseeable future, I would be a foreigner – an *extranjero* – in a land with a checkered history, where I barely spoke the language.

It all started, six years earlier, with an email. It was the kind of email that would trip up most spam filters. I wasn't being offered true love, millions of dollars from an offshore bank account, or improved performance in bed. I was being offered a book deal.

I had never thought of myself as a writer. In fact, I hated writing as a kid. As I considered accepting that book deal offer, every author I talked to warned me: "Writing a book is extremely hard work, with little chance of success." But I figured, *How hard can it be?*, and signed my first literary contract.

I DIDN'T know how to write a book, but the most obvious method was: time management. I needed to make sure I had the time to write the book.

In an attempt to meet my tight deadline, I used every time management technique I could think of. I scheduled writing sessions on my calendar. I developed a morning routine to start writing as quickly as possible after waking up. I "time boxed," to limit the time I would spend on pieces of the project.

Still, I didn't have enough time. I fired my clients. I cancelled dates and turned down party invitations. I started outsourcing my grocery shopping, my meal preparation, even household chores. If there was anything I had to do myself, I made sure to "batch" it into blocks of time when I could do it all at once.

Writing the book became my one and only focus. I

cleared away any time I could, and I dedicated it to writing. But it still wasn't enough. I spent most of my day hunched over my keyboard, rocking back and forth in agony. I felt actual physical pain in my stomach and chest. My fingers felt as if they had been overtaken by rigor mortis. I struggled to write even a single sentence. I was spending plenty of time on my book, but I wasn't getting anything done.

MY CASE of writer's block was so bad that, weeks after signing my contract, I accepted a last-minute invitation to go on a retreat to Costa Rica. Logically, it wasn't the best use of my time, but I desperately hoped that a change of scenery would work some kind of magic.

A few days into the trip, I was more worried than ever. According to my contract, if my manuscript wasn't twenty-five percent finished within a few weeks, the deal was off. Yet I still hadn't written a single word. Unless a miracle happened, I would write a check to the publisher to return my advance, and I would humiliatingly face my friends, family, and blog readers to tell them I had failed. Does that sound like a lot of pressure? It was.

I went for a walk, so I could feel sorry for myself, by myself. I was dragging my feet down the gravel road, head hung down and arms crossed over my chest. *How could I be so foolish?*, I wondered. Not only had I committed to writing a 50,000-word book – with detailed illustrations – despite having little writing experience beyond a few blog posts, but I had wasted time and money going on this retreat.

Then, I heard someone call out. I looked up, and on the next road over was a man waving and yelling, *¿¡Como estáááás!?* I had briefly noticed the man moments before. His fists had been wrapped around the simple wires of a fence, his arms stretched out in front of him as he leaned back in ecstasy, singing to himself. I had felt vaguely embarrassed for him, assuming he didn't know someone else was around.

As the man motioned for someone to come to him, I hesitated. It looked as if he was motioning to me, but that seemed unlikely. Yet I looked around, and saw nobody.

I had just passed a fork in the road, and the fence the man stood behind was on the other side of the fork. I didn't want to backtrack, because I felt I should return to the house and try to write. But I felt rude for ignoring his friendly invitation. So, still not sure what he wanted, I reluctantly retraced my steps and walked over to the man.

What followed was the first conversation I ever had entirely in Spanish. Though, I'm using the word "conversation" loosely. The man – Diego was his name – taught me the words for the sun, the beach, the rain and the sea. It turned out Diego just wanted to chat.

My conversation with Diego was refreshing. I was used to everyone ignoring each other on the crowded streets of Chicago, but here was a man who wanted to talk to someone on the next road over about nothing in particular. I was suddenly in such a relaxed state of mind that, after bidding Diego farewell, it was several minutes before I noticed I was going the wrong way. I had continued down Diego's side of the fork in the road. When I realized this, I panicked at the prospect of getting lost in a foreign country, but then I shrugged it off and decided to keep going. It turned out I got back to the house just fine anyway.

Between the pep talk I had gotten from my friend Noah Kagan – as described in my book, *The Heart to Start* – and my conversation with Diego, I felt as if I had turned over a new leaf. I set my laptop on a desk in the interior balcony of the house. There, looking out at the sapphire blue Pacific Ocean, I had my first breakthrough writing session. What once seemed impossible, now seemed easy. After an hour of writing, I had most of a chapter drafted. It suddenly seemed as if I might make my deadline after all.

THAT RANDOM conversation on a gravel road in Costa Rica became the seed of an idea that would eventually drive me to sell everything I owned and buy a one-way ticket to South America.

I had discovered that making progress on my first book wasn't so much about having the time to write. It was about being in the right state of mind to do the work at hand. I had discovered that today's productivity isn't so much about time management as it is about mind management.

WELCOME TO THE CREATIVE AGE

The shift didn't happen overnight. Throughout the course of writing my first book, I still got stuck all the time. But it became abundantly clear that I had picked the low-hanging fruit in managing my time. There were instead opportunities to be more productive, with less pain, in managing my mind.

After all, why was it that I was banging my head against the wall twelve hours a day? Why was it that, seemingly out of nowhere, I would suddenly start making progress? Sometimes, I would do an entire day's writing in only fifteen minutes. The only problem was, I had to sit at my keyboard all day to find that fifteen-minute window in which writing would suddenly come easily.

If only I could sit down, do that fifteen minutes of writing, and get on with the rest of my day!, I thought.

I'm sure you've experienced this before. You were working hard on something, but not making progress. Maybe you were writing a book, maybe you were learning a language, or maybe you were simply making a tough life decision. You kept pushing, but it felt as if you were getting nowhere. You abandoned the project multiple times. But then, as you were on the edge of burning out, everything clicked. You had a fruitful writing session, you suddenly understood your new language, or that decision that once seemed impossible now seemed easy.

Writing my first book was a creativity pressure cooker. That's what it took for me to realize that I needed to manage my mind, instead of my time. But as I reflected on the experience, I saw that this also applied to other aspects of my life and work. In my career as a designer, I had often spent weeks thrashing about, sure I would never reach a solution – only to have that solution appear out of nowhere. As an entrepreneur, I had struggled to choose a direction, only to have the best choice become clear after "sleeping on it." As a marketer, I had agonized over how best to expend limited resources, only to later feel confident about my cohesive plan. I could see parallels in learning to dance Salsa, play guitar, or speak Spanish – even in making big life decisions. Most people's idea of productivity is to be able to produce a lot of something. To *do* a lot. Follow a series of steps, and you're done. Do it over and over again.

But, more and more, if it can be completed in a series of steps, there's no point in doing it. AI and automation are poised to eliminate forty to fifty percent of jobs within the next decade or two. It's the jobs in which people follow a series of steps that are the most at-risk. AI expert Kai-Fu Lee says it's the "optimization-based" jobs that will be taken over first. Jobs such as loan underwriters, customer service representatives, even radiologists. Jobs that involve what Lee calls "narrow tasks," such as finding the ideal rate for an insurance premium, maximizing a tax refund, or diagnosing an illness. Tasks involving optimizing data will be the first to go.

Which jobs are safe from the reach of AI? According to Lee, it's the jobs that require creativity.

When many people think of "creativity," they think of watercolor paintings or macramé. But creativity expands way beyond those examples. Scientists who study creativity define it as coming up with something both novel and useful.

According to Lee, if you have to think across different subjects, if you work in an "unstructured environment," or if the outcomes of your work are hard to measure, the work you do will be relevant far into the future.

These days, the mental work that matters isn't about

following a series of steps. It's about finding your way to a novel and useful solution.

EACH NOVEMBER, aspiring writers set out to write a novel – the book kind of "novel" – in a month. It's a collective event called NaNoWriMo, short for National Novel Writing Month. Since 2013, in parallel to NaNoWriMo, computer programmers have been participating in NaNoGenMo – National Novel Generation Month. They try to generate novels using code.

In the 2019 NaNoGenMo, some novels were written by an AI model once considered too dangerous to be released to the public. Yet the novels were still not even close to making sense. In fact, this AI model could hardly write a coherent sentence. AI expert Janelle Shane tweeted, "Struggling with crafting the first sentence of your novel? Be comforted by the fact that AI is struggling even more." The sentence this AI model generated for Janelle: "I was playing with my dog, Mark the brown Labrador, and I had forgotten that I was also playing with a dead man." Not exactly Tolstoy.

You can type 50,000 words in a day. A computer can generate 50,000 words faster than you can blink. Yet, you can think up a 50,000-word novel in about a month. A computer can't do it at all.

Your edge as a human is not in doing something quickly. No matter how fast you move, a computer can move faster. Your edge as a human is in thinking the thoughts behind the doing. As entrepreneur and investor Naval Ravikant has said, "Earn with your mind, not your time."

This is true if those thoughts become the words in a novel, or if those thoughts help you learn a new skill that you add to your repertoire. It's true if you're an entrepreneur building a world-changing startup, or a social worker helping a family navigate the benefits available to care for an aging parent.

YET MANY of us approach productivity today as if it's the speed of production, not the quality of our thinking, that matters.

You could trace this attitude back to Frederick Taylor. More than a century ago, Frederick Taylor revolutionized productivity. Today, the remnants of "Taylorism" – as his methods came to be known – are ruining productivity.

THE END OF TIME MANAGEMENT

As the nineteenth century was turning to the twentieth century, Frederick Taylor grabbed a stopwatch. He stood next to a worker, and instructed that worker on exactly how to pick up a chunk of iron. *Bend in this way, grab the iron in this way, turn in this way.* Over and over, Taylor tweaked the pre-scribed movements, until he had the perfect combination of movements for moving a chunk of iron efficiently.

As if he were programming computers, Taylor then taught those prescribed movements to the other workers in the yard of Bethlehem Steel. Their productivity skyrocketed. It quadrupled, in fact. "Scientific management," aka "Taylorism," was born.

Taylorism swept through the industrial world, and brought productivity forward by leaps and bounds.

What we now think of as "time management" is a child of Taylorism. Before Taylorism, workers weren't thinking about time. When most of the population was working on farms, they weren't deciding what to do and when to do it based upon the movement of a stopwatch hand. They were asking themselves when the sun would rise or set, when it would rain, or when the first frost would come. When would the cornstalks be up to your knees or waist or chin? These questions were not questions of seconds or minutes or even hours. They were questions of days and weeks and sometimes months or years. Most of the day, most people didn't even know what time it was.

Taylor's big contribution to productivity was that he thought of time as a "production unit." Add more time, get more output. Add more work within that time, get more output. What Taylor did was fill the available time with the most efficient movement possible. When he taught those movements to every worker in the steelyard or in the factory, it made them more productive.

Today, we still think of time as a "production unit." This attitude is so ingrained in our culture that we're hardly aware of it. It's the "water" that we, the fish, swim in. We wake up to an alarm – we've tweaked our wake-up time so that we can wake up as late as possible, and still get to work on time. As we drive to work, our navigation system calculates exactly how long it will take – given the traffic conditions – for us to arrive. At work, we diligently fill out our time sheets, so our employer can bill clients for our time. If you're reading this book on an e-reader, there's probably an estimate at the bottom of the screen telling you how long it will take to finish this chapter. Everything around us is set up with the assumption that time is extremely valuable. That whatever your goal, if you reach it in less time, that's a good thing. That if you spent time on something, that means you performed a valuable service. "Time is money," as they say.

But there's something we're forgetting when we treat time as if it were money. Even Taylor knew this fundamental truth. It's that any "production unit" has its limits. Exploit any resource enough, and you'll eventually stop getting benefits.

Taylor was filling his workers' time with efficient movement. But Taylor noticed that if he tried to fill *all* of his workers' time with efficient movement, he didn't get what he expected. If he wanted to get a full day out of a worker who was moving chunks of iron in the yard, Taylor needed not only to prescribe movement to that worker – Taylor also needed to prescribe rest to that worker.

So, at some point, time was no longer the only resource for Taylor to optimize. Taylor had to leave some time empty to truly get optimal output from his workers.

There's a concept in economics known as "the point of diminishing returns." That's the point at which each additional production unit doesn't get you the same output as the previous production unit. Say your worker moved five chunks of iron in ten minutes. In the next ten minutes, he only moves four chunks of iron. The worker is tired, and can't keep up. The *return* you're getting for each additional production unit is *diminishing*.

There's a further concept in economics beyond the point of *diminishing* returns. It's the point of *negative* returns. This is where the additional production unit doesn't just bring you lower returns than the previous production unit – it actually causes your total output to be *less* than if you had not added that production unit at all. Say instead of the worker moving five chunks of iron in ten minutes, you order him to move an incredible eight. But after an hour of working at this pace, the worker collapses on the floor. If you hadn't been such a greedy boss, the worker could have worked all day, and moved a lot of iron. But now, he's already exhausted.

It's relatively simple to use time more efficiently when you're following a series of steps. Experiment with filling time with those steps, and you'll find the right mix of work and rest.

But in today's world, where creative thinking is key to being productive, you can't get more output simply by optimizing time.

Still, in this demanding and fast-paced world, it's as if we have no choice but to cram our schedules, to multitask, and to always be in a hurry. Any opportunity we can find to do things faster, with less waiting, or to "kill two birds with one stone," we have to take it.

This has driven us to "time worship."

TIME WORSHIP

Time has become our "God value." Author Mark Manson describes a God value as the "top of our value hierarchy," and "the lens through which we interpret all other values." Our God value is the most important factor by which we decide to choose one thing over another.

As time worshippers, saying "yes" to a meeting invitation that fills empty space on our calendar is clearly better than leaving that space empty. More events in less time is better, and we can't imagine what we'd do with empty space on our calendar.

As time worshippers, struggling once again to speed read seems worth it, because moving your eyes over more words in less time is clearly better than moving your eyes over fewer words in more time. Never mind if we immediately forget what we've just read, never apply it to our lives, and kill any pleasure we once took in the act of reading.

As time worshippers, when we're multitasking, it at least *feels* as if we're doing more things in less time – even if research shows we're merely wasting time and energy switching between tasks over and over.

Our time worship drives us to do strange things to save time. There's an app called Exit Strategy, which helps New Yorkers save time while riding the subway. Exit Strategy shows you which subway car to get on so that when you reach your destination – wait for it: you can exit the station faster. It sounds like an obscure idea, but Exit Strategy has earned its developer a small fortune.

In my college dorm, I had a neighbor who was running every time I saw him. The first time I saw him, I thought he must be in a rush. But the hundredth time, I figured something must be up. When I finally did get to ask him – when he wasn't running – why he was always running, he reasoned: "It saves time." Not surprisingly, he was an engineering major.

I'm no stranger to employing weird tactics myself in order to save time. Are you ready for this? I've actually taught myself to press the elevator button for my floor – like a no-look pass – by looking in the mirror in the back of my apartment building's elevator. I save a tiny amount of time because I don't have to turn around before I press the button.

Saving time is not without value. According to Exit Strategy, burying your face in their app will "shave *minutes* off

every subway trip" (emphasis mine). I estimate that my inge-
nious no-look elevator button press saves me a grand total of
two seconds a week. I suppose my neighbor did save time –
and got exercise – while running all over campus, but what
did he do if he saw a friend? Decide that stopping and
talking for a minute would be a waste of time?

To each their own, but time worship permeates American culture, affecting the way others treat you, no matter
how much you try to forget about time: That friend who
always shows up late because he can't risk being early. The
waiter who slams down the check before you've finished
chewing your last bite, then hovers over your table impa-
tiently. The woman behind you in line at the supermarket
who loudly groans after you commit the mortal sin of
stealing three seconds from her day by dropping your credit
card. The root of all of this incivility lies in praying to the
false God of time.

When you choose a "God value," all your decisions
optimize for one thing, at the expense of everything else.
What other things could you think about or do while leaving
a subway station at a normal pace? What valuable college
relationships did my neighbor miss out on by running all the
time? Which neighbors would invite me to parties if I didn't
make a fool of myself in the elevator?

You can cut calories toward a healthy diet, but at some
point you've cut too many calories. You can save time toward
a productive life, but at some point you've cut too much *life*.
Thirty percent of working Americans are apparently so
short on time that they now get less than six hours of sleep.

That reduction from the recommended eight hours is not only enough to kill their creativity, it also increases their risk of high blood pressure, diabetes, obesity, cancer, and other serious illnesses. Additionally, it leaves many with no choice but to consume copious amounts of caffeine, driving a downward spiral of less restful sleep, stunted memory formation, and further health risks.

WHEN YOU SAVE TIME, KEEP IT

As desperate as we are to get more out of our time – as if our hourglasses were filled with golden dust – it's surprising how little respect our culture has for time. People are actually offended if you leave time unplanned for, unused, or empty. We say people with time-consuming hobbies or interests have "*too much* time on their hands." While that time is on their hands, apparently they should fight it – perhaps by using the practice of "time *boxing*." If they still can't pound something productive into the empty time on their schedule, they should do more than fight time. They should "kill" time.

Yet when someone has the opportunity to steal some of our time, they change their tune. We have the gall to refer to unused time as "free" time. Do we call our unused money "free" money? No! Ironic, in a world where "time is money."

Time is apparently money when your boss is using it, yet somehow it's "free" time when it's leftover for you to use. Most companies allow coworkers to see each others' calendars, for the sake of seeing that unused time. That way, others can fill gaps in our day by scheduling meetings. Entrepreneur and author Jason Fried cleverly calls it "calendar

Tetris." Our time is "free" for them to take. This practice is so widespread, there's now an app called Look Busy, which fills your calendar with fake events, so your coworkers can't steal more of your time.

This flippant regard for people's time is perpetuated by the false notion that time is a commodity. Time management wisdom will tell you that once time has passed "you can't get it back."

Here comes a counterintuitive concept, so you might need to read it twice: Time you don't use now pays dividends in the future. Consider that Bill Gates came to the realization that Microsoft should create its first web browser during one of his "think weeks" in a secluded cabin, or that Google's greatest products – including Gmail and AdSense – were created during the "20% time" when engineers could work on whatever they wanted.

If those examples are still too industrious to convince you, consider that Stephen King recommends novelists put their first draft in a drawer for six weeks before daring to review it, that Elizabeth Bishop took such long breaks on projects that twenty years elapsed between her starting and finishing one of her poems, and that Malcolm Gladwell says "the first task of a writer is to create enough space and time for writing to emerge." *Catch 22* author Joseph Heller would often lie down and "just think about the book all afternoon – daydream, if you will." George Carlin recommended that everyone do a little daydreaming. "Just sit at the window, stare at the clouds," he said. "It's good for ya." His own advice helped him become one of the greatest stand-up comedians ever, by anyone's estimation. Or, consider that Marisol would sit so still for hours at a time – like one of her sculptures – that spiders built webs between her arm and torso *on a regular basis*. As *The Color Purple* author Alice Walker said, "In order to invite any kind of guest, including creativity, you have to make room for it."

When we have extra money, we save a "nest egg." That nest egg will earn interest and become more valuable in the future. As these examples clearly illustrate, the time we leave unused in the present can have the same effect. Time spent doing nothing today reaps benefits tomorrow. So, when you save time, keep it.

Clearly, our use of time management has surpassed the point of diminishing returns – and the point of negative returns. To do the creative thinking we need in today's world, we need a different way of getting things done.

THE TWO FALSE ASSUMPTIONS OF TIME MANAGEMENT

The "time management" paradigm makes two false assumptions that are at odds with what it means to be productive in today's world.

The first false assumption time management makes is that time management treats time as a commodity. "Everyone has the same twenty-four hours in the day," you'll hear people say. It's as if you could line up those hours like bushels of corn, or blocks of frozen orange juice concentrate – each unit the same as the previous unit. But that's far from true.

A few years after writing my first book, I worked with

behavioral scientist and *Predictably Irrational* author Dan Ariely. Dan wanted to use his behavioral science knowledge to design a productivity app, with the guidance of my early theories on mind management. (We later sold the app to Google, where some of the features we came up with became a part of the Calendar app.)

One observation that quickly became clear to us is that when you look at each of those twenty-four hours in a day, one unit of time is very different from another unit of time. Rhythms within our bodies and within the world around us make each hour different from the next. Some hours are better for thinking analytically. Other hours are better for thinking creatively. As I'll explain in the following chapters, all hours are not created equal.

The second false assumption that time management makes is that being productive is about producing. "Producing" is right there in the word "productive." Time management in its most basic form is about producing the maximum output in the minimum time.

Yet the impact of what you produce in one minute can vary greatly when compared to the impact of what you produce in the next minute. The impact of one product versus another can be night and day.

You could write a novel that sells zero copies, or you could write a novel that sells a million copies. You could start a business that fails, or you could start a business that changes the world. You could create a marketing plan that doesn't move the needle, or you could create a marketing plan that puts your product on the map.

The *time* you spend on one result versus another may be exactly the same. You can work just as hard on the novel that sells zero copies as the novel that sells a million copies. Both novels may have the same number of words. Both novels may be free of misspellings and grammar mistakes. The thing that determines whether what you produce does extraordinarily well or extraordinarily poorly is the quality of your ideas.

When you're moving chunks of iron, you can easily connect the work with the results. You pick up the iron, and you've moved it closer to its destination. But when you look at how ideas happen, you can't connect the quality of those ideas to the time you spend on them. Yes, with any novel, you're going to have to spend some time moving your fingers on the keyboard. But the juicy idea behind the novel that sells a million copies may come out of nowhere.

Neuroscientists can give people a creative problem to solve. In an instant, as I'll talk about more in the next chapter, those people can go from having made no progress on the problem, to solving the problem. You can see the "aha" moment in their brains. It takes no time to have an idea, yet you have that idea in that instant because of things you did long before. Just ask opera singer Marian Anderson, who said – when learning a new piece of music – "What has appeared useless labor for days becomes fruitful at an unpredictable moment."

In creativity, unlike in moving chunks of iron, action and result are hard to connect. Maybe your brain is better-suited to having an idea because you took a vacation last month.

Maybe it's because you got a massage a couple days ago. Right before you had the idea, a woman walked by wearing a funny-looking hat, and that sparked the moment of insight. Yet the true seed of the idea may be a book your mother read to you when you were five. The idea appeared to come randomly, but your past knowledge and experience, mixed with the right mental conditions, set the stage for the idea to happen. As the great sculptor Constantin Brancusi said, "Things are not difficult to make; what is difficult is putting ourselves in the state of mind to make them."

Being productive today isn't about typing faster so you can write more words in less time, or shoehorning as many meetings into your schedule as possible. Like planting a seed in nutrient-rich soil, and feeding it the water and sunlight it needs in order to grow, today's productivity is about creating the conditions within your mind to have valuable thoughts. Being productive today isn't about time management, it's about mind management.

BEYOND TIME MANAGEMENT

Fortunately, some productivity experts have taken us beyond the time management paradigm, recognizing that not all time is created equal, and that you can get wildly different results from the same time investment. You can prioritize what you will and won't spend time on with the "Eisenhower method" of choosing the not-urgent-but-important over the urgent-but-not-important, as made famous by Steven Covey's *7 Habits of Highly Effective People*. You can choose to do the few things that bring you most of the results, using the

"80/20" or "Pareto" principle, as popularized by Tim Ferriss's *The 4-Hour Work Week*. You can cut out all but the most
essential things in life, as espoused in Greg McKeowan's
Essentialism.

Additionally, some experts have already built the founda-
tion for mind management. My personal favorite productivity system, David Allen's *Getting Things Done*, helps free up
your creative energy by putting all the inputs in your life into
a "trusted system." It's what Maura Thomas would call
Attention Management. More recently, Cal Newport identified
that in an age with unprecedented sources of distraction, it's
those who can cultivate *Deep Work* who will get an edge.

All these ways of thinking about productivity are valuable in their own way. Even time management is valuable, up
to a point. But mind management picks up where all these
methods leave off. Time management optimizes the resource
of time. Mind management optimizes the resource of creative energy.

Consider this passage from *Getting Things Done*. It's what
Allen calls "The Four-Criteria Model for Choosing Actions
in the Moment," which is a method for deciding what task
you can do at any given moment: "At 3:22 on Wednesday,
how do you choose what to do? At that moment there are
four criteria you can apply, in this order: context, time available, energy available, and priority."

Yes, in any given moment, when you're deciding what
you can get done, the "context" is important. For some
things, you need a computer. Other things, you can do on
your phone, while standing in line. Another factor determin-

ing what you can get done is the amount of time you have available. Finally, you'll choose the higher-priority action over the lower-priority action.

But the "energy available" is also critically important. Sometimes your mind is better-suited to think creatively. Other times it's better-suited to think analytically. Sometimes you're in the mood to do some research. Other times, you're better off taking care of some pesky details.

Elite athletes warm up before a big game. They wouldn't expect to roll out of bed and perform at their peak. Yet too many of us treat our to-do lists as if anything is possible at any moment. What if, at 3:22 every Wednesday, you didn't have to decide what to do? What if you managed your creative energy so well that, instead of staring, puzzled, at your to-do list, it was obvious what you should do at that time. This level of mastery is possible with mind management.

If you want to immediately get a taste of what it's like to use mind management, here's a simple exercise for you: The next time you set out to be productive, ask yourself, *What work am I in the mood to do right now?* Then, ask yourself, *What do I need to do that fits that mood?*

Too many of us live by the to-do list. We look at what needs to be done, then try to force ourselves to do it. It's no wonder why, even if we have the time, we rarely have the energy. But when our mental state is aligned with the task at hand, suddenly everything is easier. Our projects drive forward swiftly, as the barriers that once caused procrastination dissolve, one by one. If you've ever experienced the perfect alignment of mental state with activity, you know what I mean. To get into flow, you need to go with the flow.

But sometimes, something simply needs to get done now. In these cases, you can ask yourself, *What mood would be most conducive to doing this work?* Then, ask yourself, *When was the last time I felt that way?* Finally, see if you can replicate the conditions that put you in that mood. It may seem impossible at first, but just as a hand can learn to effortlessly form chords on a guitar, contorting fingers into positions that once seemed to defy the limits of the human body, you can learn to trigger changes in your mental state – especially with the help of the tools I'll share in this book.

WHY I MOVED TO ANOTHER CONTINENT

I was asking myself these questions, about my mental state and the task at hand, time and time again throughout writing my first book. Soon, patterns emerged in my process. I noticed that the right mood for certain types of work happened at certain times of day. I developed a grab-bag of routines and rituals I could pull from when I needed to change my mood. Additionally, I began to notice hidden boundaries in my thinking. Tasks that once seemed as if they were one task turned out to neatly separate into several tasks, each promoted by their own separate mood.

Once I was done with my book and reflected on the process I used to finish it, I found that much of what I had intuitively discovered was supported by the latest creativity research. I pored over books and research papers on neuroscience and psychology. The findings were strewn about, but I saw the pieces all fit together. I realized I had on my hands the beginnings of a reliable yet flexible system for creativity. Yet as I tried to formalize what I had learned and apply it to my life and work, I realized that to truly push the limits of mind management, I needed to make a big change.

One day, I was in my home office in Chicago, struggling to write. I wanted to reference an article I had written previously, so I went to fetch the link. Ten minutes later, I realized that I was still reading my old article. It sounds self-obsessive, but I have reliably found, as a writer, that most of what you write, you can't stand to read yourself. But if you've written something really good, you'll want to read it over and over again. That was what was happening. I had gotten sucked into my own writing. *Why can't I write like this today?*, I asked myself.

Later that same week, I was reading another older article, and the same thing happened. I searched my mind for the commonalities, *What separates my good writing from the rest of it?* I realized that I was sitting in Chicago, but I had written neither of these articles while in Chicago. I had written these articles while in South America. I then reflected on all my best work from the previous few years. I realized I was producing all my best work while I was in Colombia.

For the previous three winters, I had spent a couple months in Medellín. The former home of the infamous drug lord Pablo Escobar, and the former murder capital of the world, Medellín has since drastically reduced its crime rate and become a popular destination for so-called "digital nomads": people who work online, and spend a few months in one destination after another. I didn't visit Medellín as part of a regular rotation in between other digital nomad destinations such as Bali or Budapest. I merely visited to escape a couple of the worst months of Chicago's brutal winter.

I didn't know at the time what it was about Medellín that allowed me to do better work, but I knew I had to find out. At this point, it had been a few years since launching my first book, *Design for Hackers*. I had made some attempts to write another book, but I had failed.

When I finished writing my first book, I felt both an incredible sense of peace, and an incredible sense of horror. I felt at peace because I had accomplished something I had set out to do. It was a gigantic to-do item that had been marked "done." But I felt horror because I was certain I would want to write a book again. In the wake of the project lay a trail of loneliness, depression, and neglected relationships.

There was no way I could repeat that process. Still, I desperately wanted to write another book. As Maya Angelou supposedly said, "there is no agony greater than bearing an untold story inside you." Yet Viktor Frankl, who suffered the horrors of concentration camps, paraphrased Nietzsche by saying anyone who discovers their creative work "knows the *why* for his existence, and will be able to bear almost any *how*."

By accident, I had discovered the *why* for my existence – I wanted to write books. But I had already bared a painful and self-destructive *how* – a *how* that I knew was ultimately counterproductive. If I wanted any chance at a happy life, and if I wanted any chance at doing better work, I needed to change something about my *how*.

So, I set out to make the best possible use of my creative energy. To do so, I needed to move to another continent.

FROM A TIME MANAGEMENT WORLD
TO A MIND MANAGEMENT WORLD

In this book, I share a cohesive and flexible system for managing creative energy. This is my proposal to humanity to let go of the notion that we can squeeze more from our time. Instead, let's think about how to get more from our minds.

We'll start, in the next chapter, with the single building block of creative thinking – the moment of insight. If we understand what a creative insight is, and how insightful thinking differs from analytical thinking, we can know how to create the conditions for insight to happen. We'll find your Creative Sweet Spot, so you can do your best creative thinking when the time is right.

Then, we'll break down the creative process. Creative work is so unpredictable because progress doesn't happen linearly. Instead, our creative projects iterate through the Four Stages of Creativity. If we learn what these stages are, and how to create room for them, we can stop struggling to achieve solutions, and start letting those solutions come to us.

Then, we'll talk about mental states. Just as there are many hours in the day that you use to manage your time, there are various mental states that your mind inhabits. I've identified Seven Mental States that effortlessly move creative projects forward. I'll show you what those mental states are, and help you identify how to match your mental state to the task at hand, or vice versa.

Next, we'll learn how to leverage the power of Creative Cycles. You'll learn to see the natural ups and downs in the creative process, and the natural ups and downs in your own creative energy – as well as in the world around you. By timing your efforts according to Creative Cycles, you'll make more progress with less sweat.

Then, we'll wrap all of this into Creative Systems. Creative Systems turn your projects into repeatable systems – repeatable systems that are flexible enough and that provide enough space to account for the fickle nature of creative thinking. You'll learn how to design Creative Systems that allow you to do some of your best thinking when you aren't actively thinking, and that feed into one another, turning tiny actions into big outcomes.

You can plan the perfect system, but it's only useful if it can stand up to the unexpected and unplanned. In the final chapter, you'll learn about Creating in Chaos. Learn how to keep your projects moving forward when life's inevitable chaos gets in the way. In fact, learn how to recognize the creative opportunities presented by that chaos, and capture and cultivate those opportunities to make use of them the next time you're racking your brain for ideas.

I'm not a professor at an Ivy League university. I'm not a productivity consultant. I'm not a journalist for a major newspaper. Nor do I aspire to be any of these things. I'm just another creative, trying to make my ideas real before I leave this world. As with all of my books, I'm writing it to solidify these concepts in my own mind, and hopefully help you while I'm at it.

So, I'll be presenting these concepts the same way I discovered them – through my own experiences. I'll take you along on my journey, from the soaring skyscrapers of Chicago, to the rolling green hills of Colombia, to the blistering desert heat of Arizona. You'll be there with me from my highest highs to my lowest lows. I don't expect this will be like any productivity book you've read before. It will make you laugh, and it might even make you cry. I know writing it did both for me.

You don't have to move to another continent to start managing your *mind* instead of your *time*. Consider me the subject of an experiment, of which you can now reap the benefits. It would have been impossible for the average American, living in American culture, to live according to what I discovered in the process of building this system. If you want to kill creativity: Get five hours of sleep a night, fight traffic for two hours a day, and start each day with a piping hot thermos of a psychoactive drug. This is the unfortunate and inescapable reality of most Americans today.

Some of what I present may seem impossible in today's "time management" world. Consider this book a blueprint for the future – my proposal for us to ease back on our time management world, and start building a "mind management" world. It won't be a cultural shift that we can all make at once. Implement what you can from this book. One day, I dream that workplaces, schools, and public spaces will start working not according to what gets the most output out of the least amount of time, but instead according to what contributes to the appropriate mental state for what we're trying to achieve. We'll stop forcing adolescents to go to school early in the morning, when their biological clocks still want them to be in bed. We'll let go of time worship and stop making decisions because it's the most efficient use of every resource *except* creative energy. Employers will stop forcing people to work in noisy, open-office environments – vulnerable to interruptions that can break any state of focus they might be able to achieve. We'll start showing respect for the invaluable resource of creative energy.

Let's return now to the beginning of my experiment in redesigning my life to manage creative energy, instead of time. To prioritize creativity, I needed to intimately understand creativity, and to find where my best ideas lie. I needed to find my Creative Sweet Spot. It wasn't until after I moved to Colombia that I realized exactly what made it the perfect place to manage my mind.

CHAPTER 2

CREATIVE SWEET SPOT

Four hours creative work a day
is about the limit.

—G. H. HARDY

I ARRIVE in Colombia late in the night. As my taxi descends into the dark valley, the lights of Medellín form a welcoming beacon below. My building is a modern but flimsy high-rise, like stacks of glass laboratory rat cages. Claim the keys from the doorman, take the elevator up, and I'm in my new home – a tiny one-bedroom apartment.

I drag my suitcases over the shiny ceramic tiles, and collect them next to the faux-black-leather couch. To my right, there's a dining table, glass-topped with wood trim and lightly-damaged matching chairs. Two awkward oil paintings call out to each other across the lonely living room.

After the month-long task of liquidating my possessions, one simple realization helps me savor this moment: I don't care about any of this stuff. The furniture is worse than the IKEA junk I had to get rid of back in Chicago. The plus is that when I leave this apartment, I can leave this furniture here, too.

Each month, I'll pay one lump sum, via credit card, to a local vacation-rental company. That covers the rent, the utilities, internet – everything. I've arranged for weekly clean-

ings, and I don't even have to change my own lightbulbs. All
this for about thirty-percent less than I was paying to live in
Chicago.

Cheap rent is good, on a writer's budget. It's also good,
because, aside from a few regular streams of income in my
business, I'm not exactly sure how I'm going to make money.
Thanks in part to what I earned when Google bought
Timeful, I've saved up enough to embark on this experiment
for a while. It will hurt to dig into savings, but the investment
is necessary.

There's a story Stephen Covey tells in his book *First
Things First*, about a business lecturer who brings a jar to a
seminar. The lecturer fills the jar with big rocks, and asks the
class, Is the jar full? They agree that it is. He pours in gravel,
which fills in the spaces amongst the rocks. Now is the jar
full? It seems like it is, but the class is skeptical – understandably. Then he pours in sand, which fills the spaces within the
gravel. It's not until he finally pours water into the jar, that
the jar is truly full.

What's his point? When the lecturer asks the class, he
gets a response you would expect from time worshipers: No
matter how full you think your schedule is, you can always fit
in more.

But his point was not about how many different things he
could fit in the jar, but instead about the order in which he
filled the jar with those items. If he had filled the jar with
sand first, there would have been no room for the gravel.
More importantly, there would have been no room for the
big rocks. The lesson is that if you don't fill your life with the

important things first – the "big rocks" – you'll never have room for those big rocks at all. *First Things First.*

Writing has become the "big rock" around which I'm building everything else in my life. I've cleared away all my possessions, and I've cleared away as many responsibilities as I can. When I wrote my first book, I freed up all the time I could – but that turned out not to be enough. To write this book, I'm freeing up all the mental energy I can. For the foreseeable future, I don't want to think about anything other than how to manage that mental energy.

It's nothing new for a writer to search for special surroundings. Thoreau had Walden Pond. Maya Angelou rented a hotel room near her house, and even removed the artwork from the walls. For me, the surroundings themselves are part of the project – which I guess is what Thoreau was doing, if I can dare to make the comparison.

The way I think of this new life is a four-year foreshadowing of what many people experienced for the first time during the coronavirus quarantines. I'm thinking of myself not as rocks in a jar, but as a brain in a jar – on Mars. In Medellín, I can get all the basics I need. With Medellín's robust *domicilios* culture, I can usually get those things delivered – even doctor's appointments and haircuts. But, most of my work and relationships will be maintained through the internet. From this apartment-cum-laboratory, I'll publish my words to the world. I'll also make regular video-chat appointments with friends and family.

As I learned from my random encounter with Diego on that Costa Rican road, the key to doing creative work is to

get into the right state to do that work. Since writing is my
"big rock," I'm starting with that. I'll create the ideal conditions for my "brain in a jar on Mars" to write. I'll then let
everything else build around that big rock.

DIVERGENT/CONVERGENT

To begin, I'll optimize for the type of thinking I need my
brain to do. Creative work such as writing requires both
"divergent" and "convergent" thinking. These two types of
thinking are at odds with one another, so this presents a challenge.

When you think divergently, your thoughts *diverge*. You
pay attention to a wide variety of things, so you can connect
those things to generate new ideas. As the poet Robert Frost
said, "An idea is a feat of association."

Coming up with ideas requires divergent thinking, but
actually producing something with those ideas requires the
opposite of divergent thinking. It requires convergent thinking. When you thought divergently, you collected a lot of
different inputs, and you came up with options. Now, you
need to narrow those options down. You need to converge on
a simple solution.

The process of writing starts off with exploring the many
different ways you might say something. What do you want
to say? What words will help you say it? Will you write in
haiku, iambic pentameter, or use some more subtle way of
arranging the words for rhythm? This exploration of options
is a divergent process.

Next, you're narrowing down those options. You decide

you'll say one thing before you say another. You decide one word works better than another. You choose one sentence structure over another. Meanwhile, you're following rules of spelling and grammar. Rather than a divergent process, this narrowing down of options is a convergent process.

Divergent thinking is a shotgun spray. Convergent thinking is a sniper shot. Divergent thinking is a summer breeze. Convergent thinking is a paring knife.

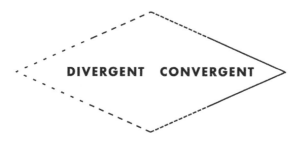

So the challenge in doing more and better writing, or the challenge in any creative work, is to balance divergent thinking with convergent thinking. You need to generate ideas, but you'll move forward with only the best ideas. As you complete your final product, you need to put on the finishing touches.

But your final product is no good unless your ideas are good, too. As you refine your ideas with convergent thinking, you need to start with good ideas – generated by divergent thinking.

So, how do I design this new life around having good ideas? I need to find my "Creative Sweet Spot."

Your Creative Sweet Spot is the time and place in which you do your best creative work. Your Creative Sweet Spot is the "big rock" around which you build the rest of your schedule and routines. The best way to manage your creative energy is to first find your best creative energy, then make the most of that energy.

A MICROCOSM OF CREATIVITY

How do you find your Creative Sweet Spot? Let's start by breaking down creative thinking into its most fundamental building block. When scientists study creativity, they often use a benchmark test called a Remote Associates Test, or more literally, a "word triad." Word triads are very simple puzzles, best solved with the help of divergent thinking. If you understand the mental processes you use to solve these word triads, you'll better understand creative thinking at large.

First, I'll give you an example of a word triad, followed by its solution. Then, we can solve a triad together.

A word triad consists of three – thus the term "triad" – cue words. From these cue words, you search for the one solution word to the triad. The solution word is the one word that relates to all three cue words in the triad. So if the cue words are: *cream, skate, water*, the solution word is *ice*. *Ice* goes with each of these three words to form other words: ice *cream*, ice *skate*, ice *water*.

Cream, skate, water is one of the easier word triads, but this next one is tougher. I'll present the triad, then walk you through solving it. I'll reveal the answer several paragraphs from now.

Ready? What's the one word that goes with each of these three words: *pine, crab, sauce*?

Let's see in slow motion what might happen in your mind when you solve this puzzle. You start with a divergent thought process. The more words you think of that go with any of these cue words, the better your chances of finding the solution word. You start by thinking of all the words associated with only one of these cue words. Can you think of words that go with crab? There's *grass*, which forms *crabgrass*. There's *snow*, which forms *snow crab*. *Crab* also goes with *cake*, *king*, *legs*, and *claw*.

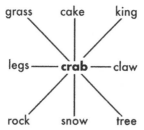

As you think of each of these related words, you're testing connections. How strongly are each of these words related to the cue word, *crab*?

There's no perfect analog in the physical world that accurately describes creative thinking. The best description at this point in the process is exploring the dead ends of a maze. As you'll see, this maze analogy eventually starts to fall apart.

While searching for words associated with *crab*, you sometimes come across a word you're not sure about. The word *tree* comes to mind. Is a crab*tree* a thing? Wasn't there a fictional character you once saw with the name Crabtree? Do names even count in this puzzle?

Now that you've thought of all the words you can that go with *crab*, you move on to another word in the *pine, crab, sauce* triad. What words relate to the word *pine?*

At this point, instead of thinking of a maze, let's look at this process as like a series of lightbulbs, connected with wires. Each word we know is like a lightbulb. Each bulb is connected to every other bulb with a wire. Some wires are thick wires. Others are angel-hair-thin wires.

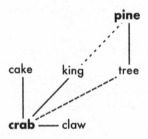

The first word you think of that goes with the cue word *pine* is *tree*. The connection between *pine* and *tree* is obvious, so *pine* and *tree* are connected with a very thick wire. *Tree* was also one of the words you thought might go with the cue word *crab*. However, remember that we're unsure about *crab-tree*, so these two words are connected with a very thin wire.

As you think of words associated with each cue word, you start to "peek." Each time you think of a word, you check to see if that word goes with the other cue words. You're not sure *crab* and *tree* are connected, so you check to see if *tree* is connected with the third word in the triad – *sauce*. There's no *tree sauce* that you know of. That doesn't sound appetizing at all. You're confident *tree* is not the solution word.

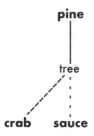

You're still trying to find a strong connection with *pine* amongst the words that go with *crab*. The wire connecting *pine* and *king* is also extremely thin. There could be a *pine king* hidden in a forest somewhere, but it doesn't seem likely.

(I'm about to reveal the answer at the end of the next paragraph. So if you want to solve the puzzle on your own, stop reading. Remember, the cue words are *pine*, *crab*, *sauce*. No pressure, though. This is a tough one.)

What I've described so far may not be how you actually tried to solve this word triad. It's only a conceptual example. If you did manage to solve this puzzle on your own – first of all – congratulations. Your actual thought process was probably far messier than this conceptual example. You didn't systematically think of every word that went with each cue word. You more likely rapidly jumped around amongst options. Then it became crystal clear what the solution word was. The one word that goes with *pine*, *crab*, and *sauce* is: *apple*. Pine*apple*, crab *apple*, and *apple*sauce.

THE SUDDEN NATURE OF INSIGHT

Neuroscientist John Kounios has observed the brains of study subjects as they solved word triads like this one. Most of the time, the study subjects solve the puzzle through a unique thought process called an *insight*. Dr. Kounios told me an insight is "a sudden realization, change of perspective, or novel idea, with an emphasis on 'sudden.'"

When someone solves a word triad through insight, they start with a thought process like the one we just walked through. They think of as many words as they can that go with each word, testing along the way. Then, seemingly out of nowhere, the answer appears in their mind. Thus the emphasis on "sudden."

We've heard tales about these moments. We may call them "eureka" moments, based upon the story of Archimedes. As the scientist Archimedes was lowering himself into a bathtub, he noticed the water rising. Seeing the water in the tub rise provided a clue that helped Archimedes solve a problem on his mind: He had been trying to help the king figure out whether or not his crown was made of pure gold. When Archimedes saw the water in the tub rise, he realized he could calculate the density of the crown – and thus the purity of the crown – by lowering it into water and seeing how much the water rose. According to the story, upon having this insight, Archimedes then ran naked through the streets of Syracuse screaming, "Eureka! Eureka!"

We also call these eureka moments "aha" moments. We associate great ideas with a lightbulb turning on. We call it a "flash" of insight. It's no wonder, when you consider what Kounios and his research partner Mark Beeman observed in the brains of study subjects, as their subjects solved these triads through insight. What they saw wasn't too different from the flash of a camera, or a lightbulb switching on. As described in their book, *The Eureka Factor: Aha Moments, Creative Insight, and the Brain*, at the moment of insight, Kounios and Beeman saw a distinct burst of activity – like a camera flash – on the right side of the brain.

This sudden nature of insight is what makes it hard to find an analog to creative thinking in the physical world. Remember that exploring the potential connections amongst the words in a triad was a bit like exploring the dead ends of a maze. But imagine this isn't your typical maze. A maze has a single exit, and a single path to reach that exit. Having an insight is like solving a maze that doesn't have a single exit. Instead, each relevant "dead end" has a sort of "beam-me-up-Scotty" portal in it. To solve the maze, you need to stand in all of these portals at once. Then the portals suddenly and simultaneously "beam you up" to the solution. It's not until you think of *apple*, while at the same time combining it with the cue words to form *pineapple, crab apple*, and *applesauce*, that you have a flash of insight.

ILLUMINATING THE NOT-SO-OBVIOUS

But just because you have an insight, doesn't mean you have a good idea. Remember from the last chapter that creative ideas are defined as both novel and useful. Notice that Dr. Kounios defined an insight as "novel." He didn't say anything about an insight being useful. Having insights and generating novel ideas is part of the divergent thinking process. Whittling those novel ideas down to the best ones and creating something that's also useful is the job of the convergent thinking process.

We'll talk more about how novel ideas develop into useful ideas in the coming chapters. But first, let's look at how the brain needs to function for us to have novel ideas in the first place. That can tell us a lot about how to find your Creative Sweet Spot.

One novel idea that also happens to be useful is the Reese's peanut butter cup. Chocolate is not the most obvious thing to go with peanut butter. Nor is peanut butter the most obvious thing to go with chocolate. Additionally, if you're going to combine peanut butter and chocolate, what's a good form in which to do that? Peanut butter falls apart, but chocolate is solid at room temperature. The "cup" of chocolate, encasing the peanut butter, is a convenient solution. The combination of peanut butter and chocolate is novel, but it's also delicious, which makes it useful. Put them together as a peanut butter "cup," and you have a hit on your hands.

How might your brain come up with a novel idea such as combining peanut butter with chocolate? The answer will tell us a lot about the ideal conditions for creative thinking. Let's return to the lightbulb-and-wires analogy. Each concept in your mind is represented by a lightbulb. Each concept is connected to every other concept by wires of varying thickness.

Each time you think of a concept, you send electricity to its bulb, and light it up. But through the wires, that bulb also shares electricity with the other bulbs, causing those other bulbs to light up, too.

If someone asks you to think of things that go with peanut butter, most people are going to think of jelly and bread, to make a peanut butter and jelly sandwich. Because those connections are so strong, peanut butter is connected to both jelly and bread with really thick wires. So when you light up the "peanut butter" bulb in your brain, electricity also flows to the "jelly" and "bread" bulbs, through the thicker wires.

Yet somehow, the "peanut butter" bulb is also connected to the "chocolate" bulb. But since this connection isn't obvious, the wire making this connection is extremely thin. When the "peanut butter" bulb lights up, it shares very little electricity with the "chocolate" bulb. The "chocolate" bulb is hardly lighting up at all.

As you think of peanut butter, the "jelly" and "bread" bulbs are burning bright. So bright, you don't notice the light from the "chocolate" bulb. Obvious connections are the obstacle to novel ideas. Remember how *tree* was the first word we associated with the cue word *pine*? When we thought of the obvious word, *tree*, it suddenly became difficult to think of a less-obvious word such as *apple*.

If you could think of more-obvious connections less and less-obvious connections more, you would suddenly have more novel ideas. The more novel ideas you had, the better your chances that some of those ideas would also be useful.

The challenge in finding your Creative Sweet Spot is to find a time and place where less-obvious connections get a chance to shine. Fortunately, the more-obvious connections don't always hog all the electricity.

NOT ALL HOURS ARE EQUAL

One of the most valuable things I learned working on Timeful was that not all hours are created equal. If you write for an hour a day, within a year you'll have a book. But you can't instead simply write for 365 hours straight, and get the same result. The longer you write without stopping, the less and less valuable each additional hour will become. You'll become so exhausted, you eventually won't be able to continue.

Additionally, time is not fungible. If you went to the Golden Gate Bridge and made a one-inch slice straight through the halfway point of the bridge, you wouldn't just lose an inch. You'd also lose a bridge.

However, you could probably grind away a thin layer of the surface of the bridge, take away the same amount of material, and the bridge would still work fine. Time works the same way. It's not just the amount of time something takes that is important. It also matters from where that time is taken. Where you choose to take that time will affect not just that portion of your schedule. It will also have ripple effects throughout the structure of your schedule, your work, and your life.

We already keep rough mental accounts of time. We know that if we want to put more time into the "work" account, that time has to come out of some other account – maybe the "sleep" account, or the "family" account.

But how many of us keep track of time's relationship with energy? There are powerful biological rhythms in our bodies that cause our energy to fluctuate throughout the day.

For example, ever notice that you tend to get tired in the early afternoon? Many people blame it on a "food coma" from lunch. Many decide it's time for a coffee break. I remember seeing an ad for an energy drink that called this afternoon dip "that two-thirty feeling."

That two-thirty feeling is actually a crossover of two different biological systems: the circadian system, and the "sleep debt" system. All day, the circadian system is climbing upward, making you more alert. (This alertness will drop sharply at bedtime.) Meanwhile, the sleep debt system is creeping downward, sapping your energy. (If you get enough sleep, you start off your day with little sleep debt. As the day goes on, sleep debt starts to accumulate.) Where do those two systems cross over? At about two-thirty in the afternoon.

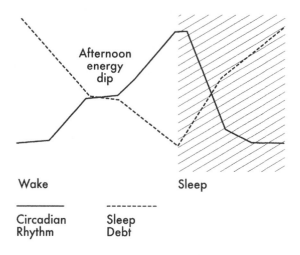

How the Circadian and Sleep Debt systems interact to cause an energy dip in the early afternoon. Redrawn and adapted from Leon Kreitzman's The Rhythms of Life.

This is why some cultures still practice the *siesta*, closing businesses for a few hours in the afternoon, to take a nap.

Additionally, you can only do so much highly-focused work in a day. When Anders Ericsson studied the practice schedules of world-class violinists, he noticed a pattern in the very best violinists: They tended to have a two- to four-hour session of intense practice in the morning, then the rest of their days were more loosely scheduled.

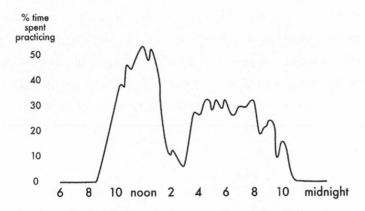

The practice habits across the very best violin players were heavily concentrated within a 2–4-hour span in the morning, followed by more sporadic practice in the late afternoon and evening. Redrawn and adapted from "The Role of Deliberate Practice in the Acquisition of Expert Performance," Ericsson et al., 1993.

This habit of intense focus in the morning is repeated so many times in the routines of writers and other creators, it's impossible to list all the examples. Amongst the endless list of morning creators are writers such as Edith Wharton, Joseph Heller, Virginia Woolf, and both Frances and Anthony Trollope. Also composers Charlotte Bray and Igor

Stravinsky, artist Josephine Meckseper, and psychologist B. F. Skinner.

Less common are the creators who work outside of the morning hours. French novelist Colette worked in the afternoons, and Tim Ferriss prefers to write at night. Some work in big sprints, such as Susan Sontag, who wrote in sporadic eighteen-hour stretches, and Edna St. Vincent Millay, who – when she was working on a book – said she worked "all the time."

I used to be one of those creators who didn't keep much of a routine. In the pantheon of great creators, that's rare. My own lack of routine is what turned out to be such an unsustainable way of working that I've found myself in South America.

To find my Creative Sweet Spot, I need to find a window of time in which I not only have the energy necessary to write, but when I'm also primed for divergent thinking.

FIRE THE CEO (OF YOUR BRAIN)

Intuitively, it seems that to do good work, we need to be alert. If we're driving a forklift or performing surgery, this is true. But creative work is different. The more alert we are, the less prone we are to doing the divergent thinking necessary to have great insights.

The most advanced part of our brain is the prefrontal cortex. This thin layer of brain tissue within our forehead does the type of thinking that makes us human. It helps us make long-term plans, prioritize, and suppress urges. It's the part of your brain that helps you avoid that extra donut when you're on a diet, or decide to cook dinner at home to save money for a trip to Hawaii.

Neuroscientists often refer to the prefrontal cortex as the "CEO of the brain." The prefrontal cortex sits at a big mahogany desk all day and fields proposals from other parts of the brain. The prefrontal cortex keeps things running, and keeps the paychecks coming. But when it comes to creativity, the prefrontal cortex is a real spoilsport.

Think of your brain as a racquetball court. There are a bunch of super-bouncy blue balls flying around the court, each representing a concept in your brain. The blue racquet-balls are *diverging* all over, bouncing off the side walls, the back wall – even the ceiling. Every once in a while, two or more balls collide, like a moment of insight, to form an idea.

But the prefrontal cortex keeps interfering. The pre-frontal cortex is focused on the rules of the game – making sure that each ball bounces only once on the floor before hitting the front wall again. The prefrontal cortex is franti-cally running around with a racquet, smacking each ball to the front wall of the court. The intention is to follow the rules of the game. The effect is fewer collisions, and fewer insights.

To do the divergent thinking required to have insights, you need as little interference from the prefrontal cortex as possible. In fact, the prefrontal cortex is so detrimental to insightful thinking that the people who are some of the best at solving insight puzzles – are people with damaged pre-frontal cortices. Their prefrontal cortices aren't interfering with the racquetballs flying around the court. They have more collisions – more insights.

Now don't go driving a screwdriver into your forehead. You do not want prefrontal cortex damage if you can help it. As I mentioned, having insights does not necessarily mean having great ideas. Even if those ideas are great, you have to execute on them – something that's hard to do if you have a prefrontal cortex injury. But you can keep the prefrontal cortex from interfering with your ideas if you can do your creative thinking when your prefrontal cortex isn't working so well. That would be your Creative Sweet Spot.

CREATE THE CONDITIONS FOR COLLISION

For most people, this time when the prefrontal cortex isn't working so well is first thing in the morning. Most of us are a little groggy just after waking up. However, most people also immediately try to do something about this grogginess: They reach for a cup of coffee.

This slight spaciness first thing in the morning is not a problem to be fixed – in fact, it's a creative gift. Instead of trying to make it go away, you can harness it for your best ideas. This is why, as I'm starting out my experiment in making writing my "big rock," I'm choosing to write first thing in the morning. No coffee, no breakfast, just straight to writing.

Writing first thing in the morning will help me have more insights. But to truly make these morning writing sessions my Creative Sweet Spot, I can do more still. The main drawback of doing work while your prefrontal cortex is still sleeping is that when your prefrontal cortex is sleeping, you're missing out on all the good stuff your prefrontal cortex does for you.

As I get settled in my new life, I notice that my morning writing sessions are going – just okay. I'm having great ideas, when I can get myself to write. But I easily get distracted. I set up on the kitchen table. I look out over the treetops through the windows, which stretch from floor to ceiling. I find that if I can have a good idea in the first several minutes of writing, I can keep going. Otherwise, I soon find myself staring out the window. My prefrontal cortex isn't there to help keep me on-task.

I decide it's time for a change in furniture arrangements. I had resolved to make sure all my possessions fit in the three suitcases I arrived with, but I'll make an exception for one larger item. I walk to a nearby store and buy a cheap particle-board desk. The box it comes in barely fits in the back-seat of the tiny, toy-like Medellín taxis. I have to borrow a hammer from the doorman to put it together.

There's a small cove in the corner of the living area of my apartment. I slide the bookcase out of that cove, and arrange it along an adjacent wall – first unloading, then reloading the suitcase full of books I brought with me. Next, I slide my new desk into the cove. It fits perfectly. My desk is surrounded on three sides by white walls. I used to keep a messy desk, but there's something powerful about this new desk's clean stark surface, surrounded by clean stark walls. This desk is so small, there's not even room for it to become cluttered.

I know research shows that big, open spaces are good for creative thinking – not tiny desks in white-walled coves (more on that in Chapter 4). But somehow, it works. I'm still groggy enough in my morning writing sessions that I'm having good ideas, yet each time I look up to daydream, there's no window to stare out of. There's just a blank white wall. Most of the time, when I look at the blank white wall, I decide that what I'm writing is more interesting than a blank white wall. So, I get back to writing. My mental state is right for doing divergent thinking, but my plain workspace helps rein in my thinking well enough to do a little convergent thinking.

However, there's still one problem: Whatever I'm writing is usually more interesting to me than a blank white wall, but whatever I'm writing is not always more interesting to me than everything else I can do on my computer. If I lose my train of thought – which happens a lot thanks to my groggy state – I can very quickly find myself checking my email, scanning social media, or simply attending to a task that just came to mind. Remember, my prefrontal cortex is still sleeping, so it's not doing its usual job of suppressing these urges.

THE FIRST-HOUR RULE

I've almost found my Creative Sweet Spot. I've found a time when I'm consistently creative, and I've found a place to sit that keeps me disciplined enough to turn my ideas into finished products. But I need one more adjustment to truly make these morning writing sessions work. So I start implementing what I call the First Hour Rule.

The First Hour Rule is simply this: Spend the first hour of your day working on your most important project, and your most important project, *only*.

It seems too simple to be effective. After all, I'm not doing anything to prevent myself from accessing the internet. I'm not turning off my WiFi, or even blocking any websites. I'm simply telling myself to spend at least the first hour of each morning writing. Why would that work?

Seasoned travelers know that if you want a good chance of having an on-time flight, take a morning flight. If your flight is later in the day, there's a higher chance there will be a delay.

Why is that? Because the earlier in the day you take your flight, the fewer chances there have been for something to go wrong. Delayed flights from last night have arrived, crew members have gotten rest, and planes with mechanical problems have been fixed. First thing in the morning, each airport is essentially starting with a blank slate.

Life is like an airport. You start the day with the best of intentions, but then delays lead to other delays, which lead to cancellations. By the end of the day, you have a stomach full of fast food and you're sleeping on the floor.

If you start your day working on the most important thing, there's less of a chance for other things to get in the way. So don't check email, don't check social media – just get right to the most important thing. Make it a rule, and it will be easy.

How you use your energy in one part of your day has ripple effects throughout the rest of your day. The First Hour Rule is no exception to this rule. The First Hour Rule helps you start off your day with a win. You feel better the rest of the day when you've already done your most important work.

Starting your day is like spinning a top. If you spin a top off-center, it will lose balance and wipe out sooner. If you start your day on-center, you'll stay standing all day long. Using the First-Hour Rule is like spinning that top on-center.

Additionally, The First Hour Rule helps train your brain to focus. As I started off this experiment, it was difficult for the first couple weeks to follow the First Hour Rule. But, as the neuroscience saying goes, "neurons that fire together, wire together." Each time you have a thought, it makes it easier to repeat that thought. So each time I resist the urge to check my email in the first hour of each day, it becomes easier for me to resist urges in the future. Soon, it became easy not only to focus for the first hour of each day, but also to focus the rest of the day.

THE GIFT OF GROGGY

You might wonder: If you're more creative when you're groggy, why isn't your Creative Sweet Spot late at night? Better yet, why not just become sleep deprived, and you'll be a creative machine? The reason your Creative Sweet Spot tends to be in the morning, rather than at night, is that at night you may not be groggy – rather, you're likely sleepy. There's a difference.

Grogginess is an effect of sleep inertia. You've been asleep and now your body wants to still be asleep. You're not quite awake *yet*. If you've had enough sleep, in the morning you shouldn't be sleepy – but you might be groggy. You should be sleepy at night, though. That's when you've accumulated a lot of sleep debt.

Remember that to do creative work, you need to do both divergent and convergent thinking. In the morning, grogginess lends itself to divergent thinking. But the higher energy level you have in the morning – or lack of sleep debt – lends itself to convergent thinking. In fact, most people's cognitive peak is in the late morning, a couple hours after waking up. So, you can use the First Hour Rule for a session of divergent thinking, and follow it up with some convergent thinking.

AS I begin this project, that's exactly what I do. Each morning, I spend the first hour of my day drafting a blog post. I then spend the next half hour editing and publishing that blog post. This helps me follow up divergent thinking with convergent thinking. Also, with my most important task out of the way, I feel good the rest of the day, and get more done.

While the morning – after a good night's rest – is a great time for creative work, I will note that sleep deprivation is not without its merits. Studies suggest that you're more creative when mildly sleep-deprived than you are when well-rested. Like in the morning, when you're low on sleep – when you're sleep deprived, your prefrontal cortex apparently takes a nap first.

I would never deprive myself of sleep on purpose. While a lack of sleep may make you more prone to having insights, sleep is vitally important to the memory consolidation that's necessary to have good ideas. You can't connect the concepts in your mind if those concepts aren't firmly embedded there in the first place. (More on this in the next chapter.) Sleep helps store concepts in your mind, so you can connect them for great ideas.

However, I do occasionally find myself involuntarily sleep deprived due to jet lag or a massively-delayed flight. When this happens, I do try to take advantage of the opportunity. Because the sleep deprivation would hinder my attention to detail, I wouldn't expect to write a perfectly-edited and ready-to-publish article while sleep deprived. But, I will do other types of creative thinking when I'm sleep deprived. As John Kounios told me, "When sleep deprived, the kind of creativity that would be most productive would be idea generation rather than the kind of detailed analytic work that requires sharpness and alertness."

In other words, it's a good time to do high-level brain-storming that I'll revisit later. As we'll cover in Chapter 3, these brainstorming sessions sometimes serve as Illumination for ideas I can later verify. As we'll cover in Chapter 4, it's a good time to be in the Explore mental state. As we'll cover in Chapter 7, this is just one example of harnessing the unexpected to find creative opportunities. I wouldn't make myself sleep deprived, but if I'm sleep deprived anyway, I take advantage.

Within my first few weeks living in Medellín, I had found my "big rock," my Creative Sweet Spot: the first hour of each morning, facing a blank wall at my tiny desk. But I still wondered, What had drawn me to Medellín in the first place? What was it about this place that made me do my best work here? It just so happened that three weeks into my experiment was about the right time to get a reminder.

FLIPPING THE TEMPORAL SWITCH

As I said, I had already taken a few trips to Medellín, during which I spent a couple months at a time here. On each of those trips, I noticed something. It always happened right around the three-week mark.

The pace of life in Medellín is slower than in Chicago. People talk slower. People walk slower. That rule about how you should stand on the right side of an escalator, so people can pass on the left? They don't do that here. People stand wherever they like. It's usually not a problem, because it's rare that anyone walks up the escalator while it's moving anyway.

Every time I came to Medellín, I noticed a similar pattern: The first week, the slower pace of life is novel and refreshing. The second week, as I'm starting to set up my life and routines, it begins to feel inconvenient. The line at the grocery store is twenty minutes long, or the gym is unexpectedly closed for repairs. By the end of the third week, like clockwork, some massive malfunction occurs, and I totally lose my patience. But in that moment, something changes.

This time, as I'm settling into Medellín on a permanent basis, that massive malfunction involves a concert. I show up to the theater and the gates are locked. There's nobody there but a stray cat on the steps. I check the event page on my phone. It's the right day, the right place, the right time. There's no notice posted on the website. *Am I at the wrong entrance?* As I walk around the building, I meet a security guard, who tells me the concert is cancelled. The theater *esta mal.* Literally, the theater is "bad." Something is broken in the theater.

I already went through a lot to get these tickets. My foreign credit card didn't work on the website, so I had to go to a physical ticket kiosk. But the kid working the kiosk told me the system was down. So, I came back the next day, and the system was also down. (It wasn't "still" down, it was down again.) So, I waited in a nearby chair in the mall for forty-five minutes, and finally got my tickets.

At the theater, after learning about the cancellation, I go to the ticket window to get a refund for the tickets. But they can't process my refund there. They tell me I have to go across town to yet another ticket kiosk. But that kiosk isn't open today. I have to go tomorrow.

So I take the following afternoon off to get my refund. After standing in line for half an hour, they tell me they can't process my refund on my foreign credit card. I have to fill out a form, and they will mail it to the home office. I should get my refund within a couple weeks. I try my best to persuade them to give me my refund now, but to no avail.

After filling out the form, I leave the kiosk, defeated and angry. Nothing about this concert had gone right. Not the ticket buying, not the concert, not the refund. I spent a bunch of money for nothing but the privilege of being sent on a wild goose chase. (I suspected I would eventually have to call American Express and request a chargeback to finally get my money back. My suspicion turned out to be correct.)

I've been through mishaps like this enough times to know what I'm about to experience – though I'm amazed it's once again happening right around the three week mark. Standing out on the sidewalk, I go from steaming with anger, to calm as a clam. Months worth of tension stored in the muscles of my back, my neck, and my forearms begins to melt away. I feel light and free – almost high.

I've talked to other expats about this phenomenon, and they report the same thing. There comes a moment when something goes hilariously wrong. The next thing you know, you suddenly feel as if you're on a different plane of existence. I call this the "temporal switch."

WHY ARE THERE EIGHT DAYS IN A WEEK?

Social psychologist Robert Levine studied attitudes about time the world over. He noticed two distinct approaches to time: clock-time, and event-time. Some cultures operate on clock-time. They do things according to what time it is. Lunch is at this time, this meeting is at this other time, another meeting is at this other time. Cultures that don't work on clock-time tend to operate on event-time. Lunch is when you're hungry. This meeting is after lunch. The meeting isn't over until we meet our objective. If by then we're not hungry for dinner, we'll also have the other meeting.

As a clock-time native, even after learning about event-time, it took me a while to understand how to think according to event-time. The best way to understand event-time is to look at how people view the standard seven-day week in Colombia, as well as many other event-time cultures. If you make an appointment with a Colombian a week from today, they will say that it's *en ocho dias* – in eight days.

The first time I heard this, I was incredibly confused. *Today is Wednesday, so – eight days – you mean next Thursday?* To a clock-time person, the appointment is in seven days. Seven rotations of the earth separate right now from the time of the appointment, a week from now. But from an event-time perspective, it's not seven days – it's eight: Today is an event, which has not yet ended. There are six days – each day its own event – between now and the day of the appointment. The day of the appointment is also an event. That's one, plus six, plus one – eight. One week from now is eight days. The appointment will take place in eight days.

This isn't what the Beatles were talking about when they sang *Eight Days a Week*. That song was inspired by a limo driver who proclaimed to Paul McCartney that he had been working hard. "Eight days a week" was his way of saying he was giving "a hundred and ten percent." When event-time cultures think of a week as having eight days, it's because they're actually viewing each day as an event. It's a refreshing thought, really: Today counts.

When a culture is following event-time, it can be confusing and sometimes aggravating to someone used to clock-time. You can't believe you have to stand in a line for twenty minutes just to buy an avocado. Everyone else in line is thinking, *What's the big deal? You'll get there when you get there.*

When I experience the "temporal switch," I switch from a clock-time perspective to an event-time perspective. I find that my internal dialogue changes. I'm telling myself,

"Things may not work out the first time you try them, but they will work out eventually." As Colombians are wont to say, *¡No pasa nada!* Literally: Nothing will happen. What they mean is, *Stop worrying, it will work itself out.* With this laissez-faire attitude, you can't be concerned with what time something happens or how long it takes. You'll drive yourself crazy, because nothing will happen on-schedule.

These observations about different approaches to time can come off as politically incorrect. If any of this sounds judgmental to you, ask yourself: Is it because you think one approach is better than another? There's the problem!

In fact, a study by Tamar Avnet and Anne-Laure Sellier found that both clock-time and event-time approaches can lead to good outcomes. It depends what you're trying to accomplish.

CREATIVITY IS A MAZE, NOT A JOGGING PATH

If you're trying to be efficient, clock-time is the way to go. Like moving chunks of iron, if you're stacking bricks, Frederick Taylor's approach to timing movements will get the wall up faster. It's a clock-time approach. But if you're trying to be effective, event-time is the way to go. If you're trying to think of the perfect gift for your wedding anniversary, getting it right is more important than doing it quickly.

Avnet and Sellier's study also demonstrated that clock-time and event-time approaches aren't strictly cultural. Most of us change our approach based upon what we're trying to accomplish.

When you're looking for your Creative Sweet Spot, it's

better to have an event-time approach. Why? Back to the basic building block of creativity: the insight. Remember that insights come in an instant. You go from not having the solution to having the solution. As John Kounios said, the emphasis is on "sudden."

As you're trying to solve a word triad, you're thinking divergently. While thinking divergently, you're thinking of words that are only remotely associated with each of the cue words. This will take you down some of those dead ends in the maze we talked about.

The mental processes behind solving the *pine, crab, sauce* word triad might look like this.

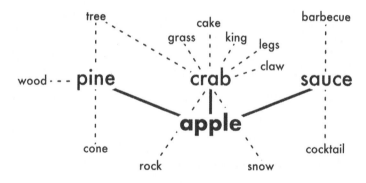

While these word triads can be solved through insight, not everyone who solves these triads uses insight to do it. Some subjects report using an analytical process – and their brain activity reflects this difference.

Word triads are a good microcosm for the creative process, but strictly analytical problems are different. The difference between a word triad like this and a strictly analytical problem can tell us something about why an event-based time orientation might be better-suited for creative thinking.

If you solved one of these word triads through an analytical process, that process would be more like the deliberate, step-by-step process we walked through together. If you first thought of a word that went with *pine*, and that word happened to be *apple*, when you deliberately tested *apple* with the other cue words of *crab* and *sauce*, you would have arrived at your solution. That would be an analytical process. You could use a similar process, thinking of every single word you could that went with each cue word, then carefully testing the combinations, and you could also arrive at a solution.

Some problems will never be solved through insight, but instead will mostly be solved through analysis. If I asked you to calculate the odds of drawing a King or a Queen from a deck of cards, you wouldn't solve that through insight. You would follow an analytical process: First you would calculate the number of Kings and Queens in a deck of cards, then you would count the cards in the deck, then you would calculate the odds.

If you happen to be a math whiz, and the odds of drawing a King or Queen simply appears in your mind, that's not the same as insight. That would simply be intuition. Your deep experience in solving math problems may help you solve them almost instantly.

Notice that the process of solving a purely analytical problem is different from the process of solving an insightful problem. When you're solving an analytical problem, you're following a series of steps. With each step, you're getting closer to the solution. You can break down an analytical problem into shifts. You could count the number of Kings and Queens in a deck, hand that off to the night-shift worker who counts the cards in the deck, then come back in the morning to make the final calculation.

The process is linear: You add four Kings to four Queens to get eight possible cards. Divide that by fifty-two cards in a deck, and you get the odds: A fifteen percent chance of drawing a King or a Queen from a standard deck of cards.

$$\underset{\text{KINGS}}{4} + \underset{\text{QUEENS}}{4} = 8 \div 52 = 15\%$$

Notice this is different from the thought process for solving the word triads, where we had to go down many "dead ends." To solve a problem through insight, you need to go down many different paths, not knowing when you'll reach your destination. To solve a problem through analysis, you go down one path, one step at a time. If insightful thinking is a maze, analytical thinking is a jogging path.

You can imagine how a clock-time orientation would be more compatible with analytical thinking. Like a jogging path, there are steps to follow, so you can estimate how long each of those steps will take. By contrast, you can see how an event-time orientation would be more compatible with insightful thinking. You have to go down many dead ends to solve the maze. When you finally do reach a solution, it will be sudden. But when will that happen? It's hard to predict.

Additionally, research suggests that an event-time orientation promotes a positive mood. When you're in a positive mood, you can more easily have insights. Avnet and Sellier's research on people who think in event-time, versus people who think in clock-time, found that event-time people are better able to savor positive emotions. They're not watching the clock, thinking of what they're going to do next and at what time. They're in the moment. If the general mood of people in Medellín is any indication, event-time does make you happier. An observation I hear over and over from Americans who visit here is that the people are in a good mood. As Demir Bentley of Lifehack Bootcamp says, "One thing I love about living in Medellín is that the people just seem happier."

The culture in many companies kills creativity. There are tight deadlines, so you're watching the clock, trying to fit the work you need to do into the time you have available. This creates a sense of what scientists call "time pressure" – the feeling that you don't have enough time to do what you need to do. In everyday life, we call it being busy.

THE HIGH INTEREST RATE OF BORROWED TIME

A Harvard study found that the busier knowledge workers were, the less creative they were. You might think that as time gets filled up with work, you simply do more of the same kind of work. But this study found that as workers became more busy, they did less creative-thinking activities, such as brainstorming. They reported fewer insights and their work was also rated as less creative by their colleagues.

But the negative effects of busyness on creativity didn't climb steadily. Instead, at the more extreme levels of busyness, their creativity dropped sharply. If they were only somewhat busy, creative thinking decreased by nineteen percent. If they were extremely busy, creative thinking decreased by a whopping forty-five percent.

As we covered in the previous chapter, in conventional wisdom, the metaphor of "time is money" stops at the point where there's unused time. The thinking is that once time has passed, you can't use it anymore, whereas you can invest unused money, so it gains interest. This thinking is flawed, because having more time available increases creativity, which increases the quality of output.

The results of this study suggest yet another way that "time is money." When you don't have money, you have to borrow it. You then have to pay interest, which cuts into your future earnings. When you're extremely busy, you don't have time, so you borrow it. You're essentially charging your time to a credit card. You pay interest on that balance in the form of lost creativity. A nineteen-percent interest rate is about standard on a credit card – not that carrying a balance is a good idea. A forty-five percent interest rate? That's enough to make a payday loans joint blush.

One of the most surprising forces is that of compounding interest. With a tiny growth rate of one percent a day, you would double your money in about two months. Compounding interest of course applies to racked-up debt, too. If busyness is causing you to constantly take a loan from your future creativity, the effects can be disastrous. You take the loan today, but you pay interest in the future.

In fact, this study found that being extremely busy doesn't just decrease creativity on the day on which you're busy. It also reduces your creativity the next day, the day after that, and throughout the project. Compounded over time, you pay a big price for being excessively busy.

I couldn't go through the temporal switch until I had hit my breaking point. Only then could I make this switch from clock-time to event-time. That was when I finally had to accept that I couldn't stick to a strict schedule. After all, nobody around me was concerned with staying on-schedule. They were on event-time.

Neither clock-time nor event-time is the "better" way to approach time, all the time. If we're counting on a flight to be on-time, we hope the airline staff is working on clock-time. But if we're trying to think creatively, we're better off on event-time.

But remember that to make creative work happen, we need both divergent thinking and convergent thinking. Event-time gives us the space for divergent thinking. Clock-time puts us in a mindset that's better-suited for convergent thinking. It keeps us thinking sharply.

If clock-time is useful for being efficient, and event-time is useful for being effective, how can you strike a balance?

MAKING UP TIME

It helps to remember that the way we think about time today is relatively new, left over from Frederick Taylor's scientific management.

It also helps to realize that the idea of "time" itself is completely made up. There's nothing about the natural world that says that we need to divide the day into twenty-four hours, with sixty minutes within each of those hours, with sixty seconds within each of those minutes. These units are left over from a 4,000-year-old Babylonian numbering system.

In fact, in the days of sundials, the length of an hour varied throughout the year – an hour was a fraction of the available daylight. In the summer, hours were longer, and in the winter, hours were shorter. It wasn't until the sixteenth century that there was a mechanical clock that counted sixty minutes in an hour. To measure seconds, we had to wait another century. By the way, here I am talking about in which century things happened, but there were millions of "years" that happened before what we've all agreed was the year "zero."

The most precise time-measuring device we have is the atomic clock. It counts one second for every 9,192,631,770 cycles of radiation in the caesium-133 atom. This is one of the most reliable rhythms in all of nature – certainly more reliable than sand falling through an hourglass or even the vibrations of a quartz crystal.

Yet we still have "leap seconds." We add an extra second to the atomic clock's measurement of time about eight times a decade. Why? Because the very thing that we base time upon is unreliable. The length of one rotation of the earth fluctuates throughout the year. And don't forget the "leap year." We add a day onto the standard year every four years, to keep our calendars in sync with astronomical events. Yet it's not even that simple. We drop three "leap days" every 400 years. The next time we drop a "leap day" will be in the year 2100.

Yes, it's useful to know what time it is. It's useful to know what day it is. It's useful to know the approximate length of a human life, and to try to plan accordingly. But in measuring time, we've lost sight of the point of time. The point of time is not to fill as much life as possible into a given unit of time. The point of time is to use time as a guide to living a fulfilling life.

Using a method such as the First Hour Rule may seem a contradiction to the idea of working according to event-time. But notice that there's nothing in particular that needs to get done within that time. I've simply identified that time as my Creative Sweet Spot, and made it a rule to make the best possible use of that time. If I had an aggressive deadline I was trying to meet within that time, I would be missing the point. A deadline would create time pressure, and that would kill creativity.

For creative thinking, time should not be prescriptive, time should be descriptive. Instead of trying to fit a creative project into the bounds of a given unit of time, use units of time as rough guidelines that can move you toward the result you want. Instead of level teaspoons, it's "a pinch of this, and a dash of that." If you write for about an hour a day, you'll become a better writer. If you read for about an hour a day, you'll read a lot of books. If you meditate for about fifteen minutes a day, you'll become more self-aware. But if you try to write a book, read a book, or achieve self-awareness within a given timeframe, your plans will backfire. Don't race against time, walk along with it.

QUADRUPLING MY CREATIVE OUTPUT

After several weeks of following the First Hour Rule, I get into a rhythm. I've found my Creative Sweet Spot, and being in an event-time orientation is keeping me relaxed enough to have insights and turn those insights into finished products.

As the Medellín days melt by, I continue this rhythm. I wake up, draft a blog post in a groggy state, then edit and publish it later in the morning, as I become more alert. I'm following up divergent thinking with convergent thinking.

I don't know if it was the event-time culture, or the consistent climate of Medellín – it's known as "the city of the eternal spring" – but before I knew it an entire year had passed. Looking back on 2016, it felt like it had been a solid year.

But how good of a year was it? I decided to tally up my word count for the year. I was amazed to discover that I had published over 80,000 words in the year – the equivalent of two books!

Since volume of output in a given amount of time is not the ultimate goal, I'd be remiss not to mention that quantity alone doesn't necessarily mean quality. Though if the research of Dean Simonton is any indication, quantity does generally lead to quality. Simonton has found that the more works a creator is creating, the better the chances one of those works will be great. You can probably think of a few Picasso paintings, but he created more than 1,800. You can hum the tune to Beethoven's Fifth Symphony, but he composed more than 650 pieces to get that gem. You can picture one of Georgia O'Keeffe's close-ups of flowers. She painted

200 floral works, which were one tenth of her total lifetime output of 2,000 paintings. Only one of those floral paintings was significant enough to sell for a record-breaking forty-million dollars.

However, as I reflected on the year, I realized that along with my high quantity of output I was also producing a high quality of work. My following online had quadrupled, and my work had been published for the first time on a number of major websites. Most of these opportunities had come to me. I had simply kept my head down and kept writing and publishing. I was making money with my writing, which was buying me more time to experiment with managing my creative energy.

80,000 words felt like an accomplishment, but certainly a writer could publish more words than that in a year. This was the first year I had really focused on managing my mental energy in ideal conditions. I wondered how it compared to the previous year.

I then tallied up my word output from 2015. It turned out that not only had my online following quadrupled, my word output had quadrupled, too! I had published a respectable 20,000 words in 2015 – about half of a book's worth. But my 80,000-word year in 2016 was a testament to the power of finding my Creative Sweet Spot.

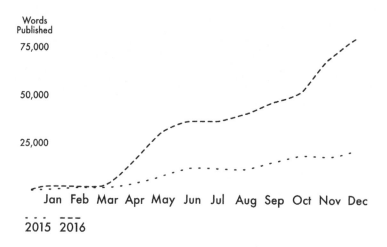

Yet it wasn't my Creative Sweet Spot alone that helped me achieve unprecedented creative productivity. My Creative Sweet Spot did help me make the most of my very best creative energy, but remember, this Creative Sweet Spot was merely the "big rock" in my new life. To really master my creative energy, I needed to also respect the finicky nature of the creative process. Fortunately, I could incorporate lessons I had learned long before.

Writing, I once learned, isn't so much about writing.

CHAPTER 3

THE FOUR STAGES OF CREATIVITY

Don't judge each day by the harvest you reap,
but by the seeds you plant.

—ROBERT LOUIS STEVENSON

F EBRUARY 14TH, 2011. Above the couples strolling along Fullerton Parkway, from the top floor at the end of a horseshoe-shaped brick courtyard building, the warm glow of lamplight bleeds from my windows, into the darkness.

Laid out across my living room floor is a whiteboard. My knees resting on the rug, my fingers search the fan of yellow sticky notes peeking from the edge of a brick-thick art history book. I open the book and splay it onto the floor, to the top left of the whiteboard.

Below it, a smaller book on typography is at the ready. To the right of the art history book, a graphic design history book. Further clockwise, a stapled photocopy of a library reference book is folded open to a highlight-striped page. Sticky notes in fluorescent blue, orange, and green are strewn across the whiteboard. Dry-erase marker lines connect the notes, supplemented by bullet-point thoughts written on the board. My living room looks like a detective's office from a murder mystery movie.

My phone buzzes on the hardwood. A friend is inviting

me to an "anti-Valentine's Day" party. To keep it simple, I lie. "Can't tonight," I respond. "Writing :-)".

In truth, I'll write very little tonight. From what I do write – in the form of notes – not a single word will make it directly into my manuscript. My laptop is nowhere to be seen. Some reference material and my own thoughts are my only Valentine's Day date.

I'M NOW almost three months into writing my first book. I've come a long way since ruminating on that Costa Rican road.

When I first started writing, I thought I merely had to write 250 words a day to arrive at my target word count. I soon learned it wasn't going to happen that way.

I won't write anything tonight, but I'm still writing. I know that I'm writing because I know that – thanks to today's research ritual – tomorrow will be easier. I'll wake up, I'll walk over the creaky boards and into my office, and I'll rest my fingertips on the keyboard. I won't have any reference material or notes from the night before. The sticky notes will be in the trash, the marker scribbles will be erased, and the books will be shut and sitting on the shelf. Still, as if by magic, my fingers will move, and words that make sense together will appear on the screen.

By this point I've learned that if I haven't done a research session like this one, the outcome will be different. A dull pain will fill my stomach. My spine and shoulders will curl forward, my teeth will grit, and my brow will wrinkle. Suddenly, something else will capture my attention. My desk will need dusting, my mouth will miss the taste of green tea, or I'll feel a chill and need to fetch a sweater.

So for now, I'm the stonemason mixing mortar, the painter stretching a new canvas, the farmer tilling the soil. I'm laying the groundwork for what is yet to come.

IDEAS NEVER COME TO A WEARIED BRAIN

In 1891, German scientist and philosopher Hermann von Helmholtz celebrated his 70th birthday. At the party thrown in his honor, he rose to give a speech. He reflected on his illustrious career.

How did he achieve one groundbreaking discovery after another? In physics, he formulated the concept of energy conservation. In art, he devised theories on color perception that influenced Impressionist painters. In medicine, he invented the ophthalmoscope. But Helmholtz was about to make one more contribution, this time to our understanding of creativity. He said:

> [Inspiration] comes quite suddenly, without effort, like a flash of thought. So far as my experience goes it never comes to a wearied brain, or at the writing-table. I must first have turned my problem over and over in all directions, till I can see its twists and windings in my mind's eye, and run through it freely, without writing it down; and it is never possible to get to this point without a long period of preliminary work.
>
> And then, when the consequent fatigue has been recovered from, there must be an hour of perfect bodily recuperation and peaceful comfort, before the kindly inspiration rewards one. Often it comes in the morning on waking up…. It came most readily…when I went out to climb the wooded hills in sunny weather.

It wasn't until years after I wrote my first book that I discovered this passage. But when I did, my experience writing that first book came back in a flash.

This was why I had learned to perform this ritual with a whiteboard, sticky notes, and books strewn about the floor. I was "[turning] my problem over on all sides." When it came time to write, it didn't matter whether I kept my notes. The "angles and complexities" were now "in my head."

I couldn't go straight from research into writing. I had a "wearied brain." Instead, I needed to wait until the morning, my "hour of perfect bodily recuperation and peaceful comfort." That's when the writing would finally come easily.

HELMHOLTZ'S SPEECH probably brings back memories for you, too. You remember times when you felt hopelessly blocked. You were writing a report, designing a logo, or trying to make a tough life decision.

You gathered all the information you could, and racked your brain for a solution. You panicked, certain you would never gain clarity. You began to question your abilities. You may even have questioned your right to exist.

But then, seemingly out of nowhere, the solution appeared. This time, the writing flowed, the perfect logo appeared in your mind, or the decision that was once unclear suddenly became obvious. It might have happened when you sat down to take another crack at the problem, but more likely it happened somewhere else. You were taking a shower, you were playing catch with your kid, or you were waiting at the check-out counter at the grocery store.

SOCIAL PSYCHOLOGIST Graham Wallas also re-
lated to Helmholtz's speech. Thirty-five years after the fact,
he formalized Helmholtz's observations on the creative
process into what he called four "stages of control." These
four stages make the random and mysterious creative process
seem a little less random and mysterious.

The first stage is Preparation. During Preparation,
you're learning everything you can about the problem. As
Helmholtz would say, you turn it "over and over in all
directions," until you "can see its twists and windings" in
your mind. You know it so well you can talk about it or
brainstorm solutions without referring to your notes.

The second stage is Incubation. Incubation is the period
during which the "consequent fatigue" of the Preparation
stage reaches the point of "[having] been recovered from."
Incubation happens any time you aren't actively working on
the problem. You could be working on something else, taking
a walk, or even sleeping.

The third stage is Illumination. Illumination is the "aha"
moment – the moment neuroscientists would call insight. It's
when the solution comes "quite suddenly." It's a "flash of
thought," that arrives "without effort." Moments of Illumination are the moments that make creativity seem so mysterious, because they are sudden and unpredictable. Your
breakthrough idea may come while making breakfast, clip-
ping your toenails, or "[climbing] the wooded hills in sunny
weather."

Finally, Wallas suggested a fourth stage, which wasn't
mentioned in Helmholtz's speech. Verification is when you

evaluate the idea you arrived at during the Illumination stage. You make sure your calculations add up. You check your facts and correct your grammar. You put the finishing touches on your masterpiece.

So, the four stages of control – which scientists widely refer to as the Four Stages of Creativity – are Preparation, Incubation, Illumination, and Verification. More than 120 years later, Helmholtz's observations still stand up. Mentioning Wallas's four stages is practically a requirement for any research paper on creativity.

WITHIN THE first few months of writing my first book – though I didn't know it at the time – I had discovered the power of working with these stages. Though I knew that I wouldn't write a single useful word in my evening research session, I was okay with that. I had tried too many times to sit down and write without doing a deep dive like this, and it had always burned me out. Thanks to research sessions like this one, I knew the things I explored tonight would connect together tomorrow.

Furthermore, I knew that the things I wrote the next morning wouldn't be ready for print. There would be awkward sentence structures, unnecessary explanations, or things I'd need to look up one last time.

My research session would be my Preparation, my night's sleep would provide Incubation, and my morning writing session would bring Illumination. Later – when I edited my writing – I would do my Verification.

By being comfortable working according to the Four

Stages, I had reduced the pain of writing. Since it was no longer painful, I was less likely to procrastinate. I knew not to push too hard to reach a solution, so I stopped burning out.

FROM THE INSIDE OUT

Robert McKee is the foremost instructor on screenwriting. His students include Russell Brand, Steven Pressfield, and Julia Roberts. Students of his screenwriting seminar have won more than sixty Oscars and two hundred Emmys.

We think of a screenplay as mostly dialogue. The only words that reach us are spoken on the screen, after all. It then follows that to write a screenplay, you simply need to start writing dialogue. But McKee teaches screenwriting in a different way. The work follows stages that aren't unlike the Four Stages of Creativity.

In his book, *Story: Substance, Structure, Style and the Principles of Screenwriting*, McKee calls this process "writing from the inside out." Instead of writing dialogue and revising over and over, the writer starts with the idea, works on the fundamentals of the story, and saves the dialogue for last.

The writer starts with a "step outline" – a series of short statements that describe what happens in the story. Meanwhile, they're also researching and writing other details that will never reach the final script – background on the biographies of the characters, about how the world in which the story is set works, and what themes will be explored through the story.

Then the writer tests the story by pitching it to friends over coffee. The writer is listening to themself while sharing the story. They're watching their friends listen: Are their eyes widening? Are they leaning forward in their seats?

If the story, as told over coffee, can hold someone's interest for ten minutes, it's ready for the next step. The writer then writes what McKee calls a "treatment," in which individual scenes from the step outline are expanded into descriptive paragraphs. Only after all this – months of work – do they finally write a screenplay, including dialogue. As McKee says, "The wise writer puts off the writing of dialogue for as long as possible."

Instead of trying to come up with a brilliant screenplay out of thin air, McKee advises his students to do a tremendous amount of Preparation. Only then can they have moments of Illumination. Over the course of many months, there will naturally be moments of Incubation – sleeping, eating, walking, or generally going about life. All along, the story is also going through Verification, as the writer tests it with friends, does background research, and examines the story's fundamentals.

This brings us to an important truth of the Four Stages of Creativity: These stages don't always progress, one after another, from start to finish. In McKee's prescribed process, you're doing Verification – such as testing the story over coffee – amidst your Preparation. You may iterate amongst various parts of the process. As I described in the chapter about "The Linear Work Distortion" in my book, *The Heart to Start*, screenwriter Jon Bokenkamp begins with stream-of-consciousness writing – which may contain dialogue. Preparation and Illumination are happening all at once.

Additionally, most creative works consist of many ideas strung together. You can't write a compelling story without many moments of Illumination. It needs to consist of one brilliant turn after another, with the characters and situation interacting to move the plot forward. A great painting may call for one brilliant brush stroke after another – each stroke representing the crook of an elbow or the leaves of a tree with breathtaking economy. It takes countless journeys from Preparation to Incubation to Illumination to connect these ideas. All along, you're Verifying your approach.

The amount of time it takes to progress through the Four Stages can vary wildly. Sometimes, it takes years or even decades to arrive at a solution. Elizabeth Bishop took twenty years to finish her poem, "The Moose," while working on other projects. More commonly, you're skipping amongst these stages for weeks or days. Yet sometimes you can go from problem to solution seemingly all at once.

CREATIVITY IS
SHORT-TERM MEMORY MANAGEMENT

Don't push too hard on creative blocks. Instead, soften them through Preparation. Why? The answer lies in the limitations of the human mind. When we come up with a creative idea, we connect seemingly unrelated concepts. But to find connections that work, we need to try many different combinations.

When we try to power through a difficult problem all at once, we limit the number of combinations we can try. We don't find a solution, we get frustrated, and we burn out. We try to use a limited amount of brain power to do a lot of heavy lifting. It's like trying to do a pushup with the support of a single pinky finger.

Our minds are divided into two parts: short-term memory, and long-term memory. We can store a seemingly endless amount of information in our long-term memory – our childhood phone number, the name of our second-grade crush, or a commercial jingle we heard twenty years ago.

But our short-term memory isn't so powerful. It can hold only a handful of things at once. This is why credit card numbers are divided into chunks of four or five digits – as we enter them into a form, we only have to remember a few digits at a time. Those numbers pass into our short-term memory, but only for a moment. As soon as we don't need them, they're gone.

WHILE WRITING my first book, I settled into my night-time research ritual because it freed up my short-term memory. Whenever I tried to research while writing, I got stuck. I know now that it's because I was trying to use more brain power than I had in the moment. I was trying to hold a lot of new knowledge from my reference material in my short-term memory.

It's no mistake that our short-term memory is also called our "working" memory. If we're trying to store information in our short-term memory, we have less brain power left over to do any other work. So as I was holding new concepts in my working memory, I was also using my working memory to test connections between those concepts. I was trying to learn new things while also trying to find novel and useful combinations amongst those things. It's no wonder I got blocked early in my writing process.

But when I spent an evening researching, it gave the information a chance to pass from my short-term memory into my long-term memory. Once new information was in my long-term memory, I no longer had to use my short-term memory to hold onto those concepts. During my morning writing session, I could apply all my brain power toward connecting concepts to form new ideas.

IN *YOUR Brain at Work*, neuroscientist David Rock compares your short-term and long-term memory capacities to a theater. Your short-term memory is the stage. Your long-term memory is the audience in the theater.

As you're trying to connect concepts to generate ideas, it's like you're pulling actors onstage to act in scenes. But the more actors you have on the stage, the more difficult your scene becomes to follow. So at some point you need to send some actors offstage.

When I tried to research while I was writing, I was bringing new actors onto the stage. These "actors" were completely new concepts – or concepts I was reviewing – so they had to come in from backstage. At the same time, I was bringing actors in from the audience. These "actors" were concepts I already knew, in my long-term memory. There was so much activity on the stage, it was hard to develop coherent "scenes."

What I needed to do was manage the stage better. I needed to exclusively bring new concepts into my short-term memory. I needed to then allow those concepts to sink into my long-term memory. I needed to bring these concepts onto the stage, like actors from backstage, and let them play in "scenes." I took notes. I experimented with connecting concepts in those notes. I sketched on my whiteboard or arranged the notes in clusters, to form a mind map. I needed to give new concepts enough space to eventually transition into the audience. I needed to let concepts in my short-term memory sink into my long-term memory.

WE BEAT ourselves up when we can't reach a solution right away. We imagine our creative heroes coming up with masterpieces right on the spot. In reality, it never works that way.

MICHELANGELO WAS NO GOD

Take, for example, Michelangelo. A famous story told of Michelangelo is that when asked how he carved the *David*, Michelangelo said, "I simply removed everything that wasn't David."

You also may have seen unfinished sculptures by Michelangelo, where one layer after another of marble has been chipped away, the sculpture emerging from the block of marble as if it were rising up from a pool of water. You imagine Michelangelo standing in front of a gigantic block of marble, expertly revealing a three-dimensional model from his mind's eye, layer by layer, like the inverse of a three-dimensional printer.

Besides the fact that there's no proof Michelangelo

actually said that about carving the *David*, you should remove this image from your mind. Michelangelo did an enormous amount of Preparation for all of his art.

Before touching a chisel to stone, Michelangelo had his sculpture all planned out. He presented his patron with a small model, made with wax, clay, or various other materials. Before building that model, he had made numerous sketches. All the while, he was drawing on a stadium's worth of knowledge to put actors on his stage. He kept a library of clay-sculpted body parts – hands, feet, torsos, etc. Many of these were replicas drawn from Greek and Roman sculptures he had studied. Michelangelo studied the human body so intensely, we still don't have names for some of the anatomical details we see in the drawings he made while dissecting corpses. His long-term memory was a treasure trove of information on anatomy, just waiting to be conjured up and mixed and matched into his next masterpiece.

There's a reason why the unfinished sculptures of Michelangelo appear as if they are emerging from a pool of water. They quite literally were doing just that. His biographer, Vasari, described Michelangelo's process of translating one of his preliminary models into a finished piece: He lowered the model into a tub of water. He then lifted the model out of the water bit by bit – using a crank and pulley – revealing one "layer" of the figure at a time. He then carefully chipped away at the block of marble to match what he saw emerging from the water.

It's no mistake we have idealistic beliefs about Michelangelo's process. The quote about removing everything that wasn't David seems like something Michelangelo would say, because it fits the public image he crafted of himself. Michelangelo was known as "the divine one." He wanted people to believe that he was a gift from God – that his genius was magical and effortless. So much so that, as Michelangelo lay on his deathbed, he ordered piles of his process work and sketches to be burned. He didn't want the world to know how much Preparation his genius truly required.

I LEARNED from my first fruitful writing session in Costa Rica that it took a certain mind state to make creative progress. I would later master cultivating that mental state in my mornings in Medellín, for moments of Illumination. But years before that, it was these nighttime research sessions that helped me appreciate the importance of working according to the current stage of the creative problem at hand.

Before doing these deep dives, the creative process felt like a crapshoot. I felt like a mouse drowning in cream, frantically moving his little legs in the hopes of turning that cream into butter, so I could finally crawl out to safety. But once I gained the confidence to truly immerse myself in the subject at hand, while being comfortable with making no visible progress at all, creating got a lot easier.

WHEN I started learning more about the working styles of great creative minds throughout history, I began to see that they all work according to the Four Stages of Creativity. Yet famous stories of creative insights still surround these Four Stages with mythology that clouds our view.

THE FOUR STAGES OF YESTERDAY

One of the most famous stories of a moment of Illumination is that of how Paul McCartney of The Beatles composed the song "Yesterday." As the story goes, he was sleeping in the upstairs bedroom he had recently moved into – at his girl-friend's family's house on Wimpole Street in London – when a beautiful melody appeared in a dream. He stumbled to the upright piano he kept by the bedside and played the chords so he wouldn't forget them. Thus, one of the greatest pop songs ever was composed.

McCartney's story is popular because it makes genius sound easy. All you have to do is sleep, and you just might write a hit. It could be frustrating to think of genius as random, fleeting, and impossible to replicate – but that, too, appeals to our lazy side. The same way people expect to win the lottery, it plays into our tendency to daydream: It's okay if we aren't putting in the time and doing the work every day – one day, we might strike it rich.

The part of the story you don't hear is that all Four Stages of Creativity were heavily involved in making "Yesterday" a hit. "Yesterday" didn't come to McCartney randomly, and when it did come to him, it wasn't ready to ship.

When McCartney first dreamt up his untitled melody he was convinced he had heard it before. "My dad used to know a lot of old jazz tunes," McCartney later recalled. "I thought maybe I'd just remembered it from the past."

McCartney did an enormous amount of Verification before recording "Yesterday," to be sure it was an original melody. At the time, there was no way for him to simply hum the tune and let an algorithm do the searching for him – as he could do today with an app. He later said that to verify that the melody was original, he "went around for weeks playing the chords of the song for people."

In fact, it would be an entire year and a half before McCartney would finally record "Yesterday." He was trying to figure out if it was an original melody, he was working on details of the arrangement. At this point the song didn't even have lyrics. He played it for so many people, and brought it up at so many practices and recording sessions, bandmate George Harrison said "he's always talking about that song. You'd think he was Beethoven or somebody."

As if he were "[climbing] the wooded hills in sunny weather," the final piece of McCartney's yet-untitled melody finally achieved the form you would recognize today while McCartney was riding the hills of the Portuguese countryside in the backseat of an Opel Kapitan. He was taking a break to vacation in a sleepy fishing village on the southern coast of Portugal – one of the few places on the planet where a Beatle wouldn't be mobbed.

It was during this moment of relaxation – as McCartney and his girlfriend, actress Jane Asher, were rolling over rough and dusty roads, past cork oak and olive trees, the sun setting over the Mira River – that words started to appear in McCartney's head. One-word verse openings were coming to him. *Mer-il-ly*, *fun-il-ly*, *sud-den-ly*, and the final name of what was to become one of the top-grossing and most-covered songs in history, "Yesterday."

After this moment of Illumination, "Yesterday" still

needed more Verification. When McCartney arrived in Albufeira, he visited the vacation home of musician Bruce Welch. He asked Welch for a guitar. It was a right-handed guitar, so the left-handed McCartney had to flip it over and play it upside down. McCartney pulled out a brown envelope with words scribbled on it and began to play and sing. Welch later recalled, "I think I was the first person to hear the song with the lyrics. I realized it was magic, with those chord progressions." Less than three weeks later – a year and a half after the melody came to McCartney in a dream – The Beatles began recording "Yesterday" in London's EMI Studios.

Like bookends, the story of how McCartney composed "Yesterday" is a story of two separate moments of Illumination. Along the way, there were countless moments of Verification and Preparation. But those moments alone weren't enough to bring the song to completion. Between those moments – and even leading up to McCartney's fateful dream – the project was undergoing Incubation.

HOW INCUBATION WORKS

Incubation occurs any time you aren't actively working on the problem. When you are actively working on a problem, you're bound to hit blocks – scientists call them impasses. If you're trying to connect concepts with one another to form new ideas, many of the connections you try aren't going to work. Additionally, you'll have loose ends – new information about the problem or potential solutions that you haven't yet tried to connect to anything else. During times when you aren't actively working on the problem, a number of things are working in the background to bring you closer to a solution.

One way Incubation works is simply by helping us forget bad ideas. When you hit an impasse, it's often because you're using too much of your brain power on connections that won't lead you to a solution. It's like a log jam. You're using your working memory to test out connections that aren't going to work. As long as those bad ideas are jammed together, creativity can't flow.

Remember when we were solving the word triad in the previous chapter? The first word we thought of that went with the cue word *pine* was "tree." But in the context of this word triad, "tree" was a bad idea. Once we thought of "tree" we became fixated on it, which made it hard to think of the actual solution word, "apple." If we had taken a break after thinking of "tree," chances are we would have forgotten it, which would have freed us up to think of "apple." When Incubation helps us forget something that's causing an impasse, scientists call this "fixation forgetting." Incubation helps you forget bad ideas, which makes room for good ideas.

Besides simply forgetting bad ideas, another way Incubation works is through memory consolidation. This is essentially getting your backstage "actors" out of your short-term memory of the stage, and into the long-term memory of the audience.

Sleep in particular helps us consolidate memories of the relationship between concepts. If I tell you that Tom is taller than Jill, but Jill is taller than Jerry, you'll better understand the implied relationships between the three after you've taken a nap or slept through the night. You'd be more likely to remember that Tom is taller than Jerry, even though I didn't explicitly tell you that. You know that Tom is taller than Jill, and Jill is taller than Jerry. Thanks to memory consolidation, you can more readily deduce that Tom must be taller than Jerry.

Relational memory – as scientists call it – is essential to making creative works. To make novel and useful connections, you need to connect concepts that seem to be unrelated. It's the deft arrangement of those concepts into a hierarchy – much like knowing that Tom is taller than Jerry – that makes a creative work evocative and interesting.

If you're writing a mystery novel, you'll spoil the ending if you reveal clues that make it too obvious who is the killer. If you're designing an app, you need to arrange the buttons on the interface to express the most commonly used and least commonly used functions of the app. If you're choreographing a dance, you need to balance and contrast the movements you choose so that some movements are heightened and others are subdued in ways that harmonize or create tension with the music. This is why when choreographer, composer, and music-theater director Meredith Monk is working on a piece, she draws charts and maps to help her process how the elements of the piece interact.

All of this requires relational memory. You need to see the peaks and valleys and learn the lay of the land before you can express only the most relevant details into a map that leads others where you want them to go.

You can't do it at first glance. You'll be too focused on details that distract from the story, or dance steps that are too on-the-nose. You need some Incubation before you reach the point of Illumination.

Studies suggest that a final way that Incubation occurs is through unconscious processing. Even when you aren't consciously thinking about something, your brain is incredibly active – something scientists call the "default mode network." You might think of it as your unconscious or subconscious mind. When you aren't consciously working on the problem, your brain isn't only forgetting the bad ideas, it's not only storing relevant concepts in long-term memory, it's not only identifying relationships amongst those concepts – it may also be subconsciously searching for solutions.

RESPECT THE FOUR STAGES

Many people dream of melodies they haven't heard before. I know I do – but I lack the musical skill to capture them and turn them into a complete song. If the melody for "Yesterday" had come to a less-skilled creator – someone without so much Preparation under their belt – the story would have ended there. A nice song you've never heard of, coming to someone you've never heard of, in a dream. But McCartney knew that completed creative works don't come out of nowhere. He spent an entire year and a half working on the song before the lyrics finally came to him.

It's no wonder that, after a morning of writing, Maya Angelou said she "[tried] to put it out of [her] mind." She created a period of Incubation. After dinner, she would read the day's work to her husband. Not to hear his comments — comments weren't allowed — but to hear the writing out loud — a form of Verification.

Ernest Hemingway supposedly said "write drunk, edit sober." Even if there's no proof he actually said it, the fact that the quote has spread says something about our collective instinct: The creative process takes place in distinct stages.

Stephen King tells aspiring writers to put the first draft of their novel in a drawer. Then he tells them to not look at it again for six weeks. He's making a long period of Incubation part of the process.

Playwright Lillian Hellman used each night's sleep as Incubation. She read the dialogue in her plays out loud each night, and again each morning, before writing again. She also did an enormous amount of Preparation. For one of her plays, she filled her notebooks with well over 100,000 words. Almost none of those words were in her final play. Years before Robert McKee had a name for it, Hellman was already "writing from the inside out."

CREATIVE PROJECTS can be overwhelming. Moments of Illumination come suddenly, and before those moments come, it can feel as if there's no end in sight. But if you're aware of the Four Stages of Creativity, you can be at peace.

Give yourself adequate time and space for Preparation, and immerse yourself in the subject. You'll be tempted to try to come up with ideas during this time. Invite the ideas that do come, but don't burn yourself out pushing through a block. Trust that Illumination will come next time you're in your Creative Sweet Spot.

Give yourself space for Incubation. Let the details of your project sink into your long-term memory. Let the bad ideas causing blocks fall away. Let your mind rank the various elements of a project so you can express them clearly. Give your unconscious mind a chance to look for solutions. You can even use Incubation strategically. You can prime your brain with clues before sleep, such as in my nighttime research sessions, or in Lillian Hellman's nightly review of her plays.

Keep the details of Verification from interfering with the creative process. When you're trying to achieve Illumination, stop yourself from getting caught up in Verification. Set aside a separate time to get the details right.

APPROACHING MY own work with the knowledge that there are stages of creativity made the creative process less painful, and more fruitful. It led to moments of sheer bliss. Despite not having much experience as a writer, there were moments in writing my first book where I felt like I was made for the process.

Yet still, there were sticking points. Times when that bliss gave way to agony, and when I felt as if I were trying to push a mountain across a river. The Four Stages made the creative process go more smoothly, yet the realities of day-to-day life got in the way. After another struggle, patterns emerged that reconciled this conflict.

CHAPTER 4

THE SEVEN MENTAL STATES
OF CREATIVE WORK

Sometimes I write drunk and revise sober...and
sometimes I write sober and revise drunk. But
you have to have both elements in creation.

—PETER DE VRIES

I KNOW the way by heart now: Descend the stairs from Michigan Avenue. From the plaza below street level, escape the stabbing wind, through the revolving door. As I unbutton my wool car coat, I turn left, then right, then walk past the gift shop. The attendant scans my membership card and directs me to the front of the line of tourists. With each step, the spaces get smaller and darker, and I get farther from the busy sidewalks and honking taxis.

The elevator is full. An older man with a camera around his neck and his wife speak to each other in German. A mother with three kids wears a Michigan T-shirt and grips the handles of a fragile stroller. A family of five discusses the oldest son's college choices. A pre-recorded message reminds me once again this is "the fastest elevator in North America." But I wish it were faster. I'm filled with a feeling of unease – as if something important yet unknown is left undone.

The doors slide open to blinding brightness. The breeze from the pressure differential propels me as I step out onto the ninety-fifth floor. As my eyes adjust, the brightness gives way to Lake Michigan on my left – a giant horizon of blue – and scattered toy buildings on my right.

I rest my forehead on the window for a minute and stare down at the tiny cars on the tiny street. I hear nothing but a soft hum where the sounds of car horns and engines used to be.

I sit at a table at the corner cafe with a 180° view of downtown Chicago. I see Sears Tower. I see Trump Tower, still under construction. I see Water Tower Place, the Allerton Hotel, and – to the West – a flat horizon that never ends. I pour sparkling water into a short glass of ice, with a wedge of lemon. I take a sip, and I sigh.

My chest is jumping, my heart getting whiplash within my suddenly stationary body. I let the buildings and the horizon close in on me. And, I wait.

WITHIN MINUTES, it starts to come. But I don't want to scare it away, so I move slowly and deliberately. I remove my black Moleskine notebook from my bag, and I wait. I place the notebook on the table, and I wait. I remove the pen from its keeping place under the elastic band. I wait. I open the notebook. I wait. I remove the pen cap. And, I wait.

Finally, I begin to write.

The words start off disorganized. A string of nonsense. Every little thing that's on my mind: *copyright permissions*, *chapter five illustrations*, *color science research*, and on and on. Then, it starts to build into longer and more focused passages. As I explore the rankings of one thought versus another, my heart calms.

Tasks that felt impossible begin to feel easy. Paths that seemed bumpy become smooth. What was a chaotic cloud of synapse fires is now arranged into strips of lights, leading the way.

I know where I'm going. I can see it all. I'm on top of the world.

NOW FIVE months into writing my first book, this is another one of my rituals: sitting at a cafe on the ninety-fifth floor of the John Hancock Center, surrounded by camera-lugging tourists. I now have a grab bag of rituals like this: My nighttime research sessions with my whiteboard on the floor. The dark backroom of Ipsento Coffee. A glass of malbec in the Kingsbury Street Whole Foods wine bar – to cap off a day of working in the balcony. A discount massage at the massage school – followed by a writing session in a cafe strangely branded by a bank. A cup of gyokuro green tea – accompanied by 200 milligrams of theanine. And watching an episode of *Curb Your Enthusiasm* – followed by an epsom-salt bath – carefully monitored to be twenty minutes long at 107°F.

Each of these rituals has its purpose. At this point in the process, the purposes are shapeless, and guided by feel. But the feelings these rituals follow are distinct. A breakthrough in writing this first book came when I discovered that getting writing done is about mind management, not time management. I also discovered that I didn't always have to match my work to my mood – I could also match my mood to my work. All I had to do was ask myself three questions: *What kind of work do I need to do right now?*, *What mood do I need to be in to do that work?*, and finally, *When was the last time I felt that way?*

By thinking of the last time I was in my target mood, I could attempt to conjure up that mood again. I might try something, and find it didn't work, but then I'd quickly try something else. Eventually, I'd find some combination of place, activity, and/or substance to combine into a ritual that would trigger the mood I was looking for.

Many of these rituals were meant to trigger relaxation, such as the glass of wine in the wine bar and the massage at the massage school. Because relaxation promotes creativity, that relaxation would then enable breakthrough writing sessions.

I also began to associate certain places with certain moods. These moods promoted certain kinds of work. The dark backroom at Ipsento Coffee was good for editing and refining my writing. The bank-branded cafe had lots of windows and was decorated in a bright orange motif. After a relaxing massage, I frequently found new, far-out ideas while writing in that cafe. And whenever I felt overwhelmed with everything I had to do, I'd grab my membership card and head to the top of the John Hancock Center, where I knew I'd get a fresh perspective.

Several years after I developed this grab bag of rituals, Cal Newport released a groundbreaking book. *Deep Work* introduced the notion that there are different kinds of work, and those different kinds of work call for different moods and energy levels. There is "shallow work," which doesn't require a great deal of focus, and doesn't call for your best energy. And there is "deep work," which is work that does require your best focus and your freshest energy. The term "deep work" quickly became commonplace amongst productivity enthusiasts.

While writing my first book, I also began to notice patterns in the type of work I was doing, and the mood that best suited that work. It went beyond "deep" and "shallow." In fact, seven different types of work – each with its own mood – eventually emerged. I came to call them the Seven Mental States of Creative Work.

THE SEVEN MENTAL STATES

My ritual 1,000 feet above the ground helped me see everything going on in my business as easily as I could see the layout of the city. A session in this mental state helped me create a plan – to decide what needed to be done, how I would do those things, and, just as importantly, what didn't need to be done. This is the first state: the *Prioritize* mental state.

I eventually recognized that my nighttime research sessions were much more than just research sessions. There were, in fact, two separate mental states I inhabited in these sessions.

The very word "research" implies that you're searching *again*. You have some inkling or recollection of the way something is, but you have to look it up or run an experiment to be sure. Instead of looking for specific information, I was immersing myself in my source material. I even allowed myself to dive into an article or a book well outside my subject area. While studying typography, I delved into the history of metallurgy, or learned about the Protestant Reformation.

"Research" wouldn't be the right term for this second mental state. This second mental state is far less-focused than Research. Inherent in this mental state is the permission to not search for a specific answer to a specific question. This mental state calls for being attuned to your curiosity, and not feeling guilty about wandering off course. The second mental state is the *Explore* mental state.

Yet sometimes I really was researching. I was searching for specific answers to specific questions I had in my mind. Questions I knew would be critical to how I would structure a chapter, or simply to getting the facts straight. For these cases, I was, in fact, in the third mental state: the *Research* mental state.

My morning writing session – both while writing this first book, and later as I optimized my creative output in Medellín – was a time to do *the work*. It's when I created what would become my finished product. I was in the fourth mental state: the *Generate* mental state.

Once I had some writing done, it still wasn't ready to submit to my publisher. I had a rough draft from working in the Generate mental state. In that Generate mental state, I tied together what I learned while in the Explore and Research mental states. I fleshed out an outline I created while in the Prioritize mental state. But now I had to take off the rough edges. I had to make sure the grammar was as good as I could make it, that the spelling was correct, and that any

facts I was unsure of while writing were filled in. I had some
of my best editing sessions in the dark backroom of Ipsento
Coffee. Somehow, that dark backroom put me in the fifth
mental state: the *Polish* mental state.

These five of the Seven Mental States make creative
work happen: Prioritize, Explore, Research, Generate, and
Polish. But none of these mental states are possible without
the remaining two mental states.

Unless you're lucky enough to have a full-time assistant,
you're going to have some pesky details that need to be taken
care of in your day-to-day. You need to change the strings on
your guitar, invoice clients, or review legal documents. Outside of your business, you need to buy groceries, take care of
family members, or change the oil in your car. In writing my
first book, I had to contact copyright holders for permission
to use their images in the book, and do my usual monthly
review of financial statements for my business. I also had to
keep myself fed, keep my apartment clean, and make sure
my bills were paid. When you're taking care of the details
that make your creative work possible, you're in the sixth
mental state: the *Administrate* mental state.

Finally, you can't be going non-stop all the time. You
need the energy to do your work. To replenish that energy,
you need to get a good night's sleep. You need to take time
off, whether that's evenings, weekends, vacations, a sabbati-
cal, or maybe just a coffee break. When I was writing my first
book, these were the times I got a massage, watched a funny
video, or took a hot bath. These rituals were relaxing, but I
chose them strategically. I knew that if I did these things

right now, they would make me more productive later. After a long day, I needed to refuel. I needed to spend time in the seventh and final mental state: the *Recharge* mental state.

These are the Seven Mental States of Creative Work: Prioritize, Explore, Research, Generate, Polish, Administrate, and Recharge. An easy way to remember them is to tell yourself, "PER Golf, PAR." "PER" stands for Prioritize, Explore, and Research. The "G" at the beginning of "Golf" stands for Generate, and "PAR" stands for Polish, Administrate, and Recharge. PER Golf, PAR.

These mental states work together like gears inside a clock. Sometimes they move. Sometimes they stop and start. But they are so in-sync with one another that the hands of the clock move forward smoothly.

The Four Stages of Creativity I talked about in the previous chapter are all about the progress of your project – How close have you come to reaching a final product? While the Seven Mental States often match up with certain stages of creativity, they aren't so much about the state of your project. The Seven Mental States of Creative Work are all about the mood you are in while doing the work. If you master working by mental state, your creative work will progress reliably through the Four Stages of Creativity.

FLAVORS OF DEEP WORK

These seven mental states tend to immediately make sense to people. At the very least, most people – if they haven't thought about it before – recognize that they aren't always in the same mental state when they're doing their work. In fact,

Cal Newport himself recently told me that, since writing *Deep Work*, he, too, started to notice mental states beyond "deep" and "shallow."

Cal told me, "The thing I learned after *Deep Work* came out – which is not really in the book, but I think is important – is understanding that there are different flavors of deep work. Not just between different professions, but within your particular profession there could be different types of things that are deep. They feel different, and there's different things to support them."

When Cal isn't writing books about thinking, he's doing a lot of thinking. He's a theoretical computer scientist and professor at Georgetown University. He told me that, upon writing *Deep Work*, his understanding of deep work was solving theorems. "But," he said, "it became clear that there are other things I do that are just as deep and require just as much concentration, but are supported by completely different behaviors. So when I'm writing is very different from when I'm reading, or taking in ideas, or having a conversation with someone who's a subject matter expert and I'm trying to build up my understanding so I can use that to develop new ideas. This is all deep work, too. But it feels very different."

You can see the Seven Mental State in Cal's work. Cal's writing would be in the Generate mental state. Reading, taking in ideas, and talking to an expert would be in the Explore mental state – or the Research mental state – depending upon whether Cal is trying to answer specific questions, or merely satisfy his curiosity about the subject.

Answering questions would be Research. Satisfying curiosity would be Explore.

Cal also has ways of getting into the right mental state for each of his different "flavors" – as he calls them – of work. When he's solving a proof, he goes for a walk. When he reads, he has what he calls "a whole arsenal of reading habits." When he reads at night, he does it in a big leather armchair. When he's reading about the philosophy of technology, he goes to a particular diner for an early lunch. There's another coffee shop he goes to for other types of reading. Sometimes he finds the reading he's doing is best accompanied by a beer.

TO BEGIN using the Seven Mental States, start with the "big rock" of the Generate mental state, and build around that. Experiment to find your Creative Sweet Spot, and build a habit out of using it in the Generate mental state. From there, gradually experiment to identify the other mental states, and be intentional about using them. Keep a journal to make observations about when you see these mental states in your own work. Throughout the day, ask yourself which mental state you are in, and match your task to that mental state. Or, if you have a task that's a high priority, ask yourself which mental state you need to be in to do that task. When was the last time you felt that way? See if you can replicate that mental state.

FUZZY BORDERS

As you observe the Seven Mental States in your own work, you will notice the borders between mental states are fuzzy.

Work that appears to belong to one mental state may actually be better suited to another mental state. One of the fuzziest borders of all is that between Generate and Explore. Some work that seems like it should be done in the Generate mental state may actually require the Explore mental state.

Choreographer Twyla Tharp starts every dance with a box. Any time she comes across something that may inspire her in a project, she puts it in the box. For example, when she created the Broadway musical, *Movin' Out*, the box was full of CDs and tapes. Twyla listened to all of Billy Joel's music, and watched all of his performances. And she put it all in the box.

It's obvious Twyla needed to review these CDs and tapes. The show was built around the music of Billy Joel, after all. But she didn't stop there. The box was also full of movies from the period of the Vietnam war, and other books and movies from that same era. The box was also filled with notebooks covering various aspects of the process: things Twyla scrawled out as ideas came to her, news clippings from the era the show would be set in, and notes between herself and the music director. She also put in the box a green beret, a pair of earrings, a macramé vest, and photographs from reconnaissance trips she took in Billy Joel's hometown.

Little of this made it directly into the show, but it was all there to inform her choices in dance, story, and costume. As Tharp herself said, "Everything is raw material. Everything is relevant. **Everything is usable**" (emphasis hers). Twyla found so much raw material for this show that by the time she was done, she had much more than just one box. She had filled twelve boxes.

As Twyla was reviewing CDs and tapes, looking up old newspaper articles, and watching movies from the era, she was clearly in the Explore mental state. She had to be comfortable with not making visible progress through the Four Stages of Creativity. Though she doesn't mention the Four Stages in her book, *The Creative Habit*, her own process mirrors the Four Stages in practice, and sometimes in language. As Twyla said, "The box is the raw index of your *preparation*" (emphasis added).

Some things that went in the box could easily be interpreted not as Explore, but as Generate. Remember, exploration is a state of openness – of being comfortable with not making progress. Generation is the state of producing something. So you might be surprised to learn that the very first thing that went in the box for *Movin' Out* was a videotape of Twyla dancing. She showed this video to Billy Joel when she pitched the show to him. Which means that before she even officially began working on the show, she had already produced choreography. Now, was producing that choreography an act of generation, or of exploration?

The creation of that initial choreography was exploration, rather than generation. Why does it matter? Because when you choose a mental state, you change the goals you have while producing the work. And the goals you have while producing the work will affect how you use your energy.

If I'm sitting down to write in the Generate mental state, my goal is to produce usable writing. There are two boundaries lying outside that goal of producing usable writing.

Outside one boundary is producing perfect writing. Outside the other boundary is producing writing that has little hope of becoming a finished product.

If I'm in the Generate mental state, I have permission to stay within those bounds. I don't need to produce perfect writing, but I want what writing I do produce to be usable. I want to know that if I later go back over the writing in the Polish mental state, I can have something ready to ship.

This means there are imperfections I can accept from myself, and imperfections I cannot accept from myself. If I'm unsure of how to spell something, if I'm unsure of the year something happened, or if I'm struggling with how best to word a sentence, it's okay. In these situations, I simply type something [in brackets], and move on. I know that the brackets will remind me to fix it later, when I revisit the writing in the Polish or Research mental states.

But if I'm writing, that doesn't necessarily mean I'm in the Generate mental state. I keep a cheap portable word processor next to my bed. First thing in the morning, I have a habit: I grab the word processor, while still in bed, and I write at least 100 words. Sometimes I write exactly 100 words. Other times, I write more than 1,000. And, when I'm done, I delete it all.

Why would I delete it? Because the Explore mental state is not the Generate mental state. If I start a writing session in the Explore mental state, my goals are completely different than they would be in the Generate mental state.

In the Explore mental state, my writing doesn't need to be usable. I can write as loosely as I want. The goal of exploratory writing isn't to create something I can form into a final product. Rather, I'm merely exercising the thoughts in my mind.

That's why I can delete the writing. I trust that the exploration I've done will resurface in some form at a later date. It's like practicing a sports movement, such as a golf swing. You don't need to record it and review your video for each stroke on the golf course. By practicing your swing, you're programming it into your memory, so you can later repeat the movement with little conscious thought.

Imagine trying to produce choreography at the very beginning of a project, like Twyla Tharp did. If you approach the task in a Generate mental state, that will result in a creative block. You'll second guess every decision you make. You haven't done the necessary Preparation to get shippable ideas. But if you approach it in an Explore mental state, there's less pressure. You're free to try things that might not work. The process of creating becomes a form of Preparation. Somewhere within that exploration will be the seed of an idea that makes it into the final product.

There are other fuzzy borders amongst mental states, such as that between Explore and Research. When you're in the Research mental state, you have a clear idea what you're looking for. If what you're looking for isn't so clear, approach your "research" in the more open Explore mental state.

Sometimes exploration can feel like you're in the Recharge mental state. You might be reading something or viewing an exhibition that's so fascinating it replenishes your creative energy.

Other times, while in the Generate mental state, you might be thinking about a higher-level plan about what you're creating – such as the availability of certain ingredients for a new recipe. You might be better off calling it the Prioritize mental state.

The mental state you decide to be in while doing a task is up to you. But be aware that approaching your work in the wrong mental state can cause a creative block.

I find that the right mental state depends a lot upon the clarity of vision I have of the final product. If I lack experience and have an unclear vision, I'll need to spend a lot of time in the Explore mental state. That will give me a chance to consider different approaches to unfamiliar problems. Likewise, if it's such a big project it's hard to picture in my mind, I'll need to spend more time in the Recharge mental state (more on why in the next chapter). If I've done many similar projects before, I can plan out the whole thing in the Prioritize mental state before I start creating.

STAY IN STATE

Switching mental states has costs, so once you're in a mental state stay in that mental state. Once you activate one region of the brain, it can take a while before you have focused activation in another region of the brain. Like a filament light bulb slowly dimming after being turned off, electrical activity takes time to dissipate.

Before I started working according to mental state, I switched mental states during my writing sessions. One moment, I tried to come up with an idea to explain something. The next moment, I tried to write some polished prose about it. The moment after that, I looked up a fact.

It's no surprise I didn't get much writing done. Instead, I got blocked. Switching mental states made the blocks worse in two different ways. One: It made me easily distracted. I didn't carve neural pathways for focus – I instead carved neural pathways for distraction. Two: It provided a convenient excuse to escape into those distractions. If writing got tough, I switched mental states: I surfed the web, and did "research." I woke up from an internet-induced coma three hours later, with dozens of browser tabs open, and no recollection of anything I had read.

This created a vicious cycle: I felt bad for not making progress. I then continued to make no progress. I then felt even worse for not making progress, which didn't help me get any writing done.

When I began working according to mental state, my productivity improved dramatically. I had deeper focus on the task at hand. By knowing what type of work I was doing, I could better settle into the right mental state. By knowing what type of work I was *not* doing, I limited the ways I could get off track.

This is the hidden value of putting words [in brackets] while writing. Yes, it serves as a reminder that I need to look something up or brainstorm something, but it has another purpose. Creating a placeholder prevents me from switching mental states. It allows me to make the most of my creative energy while in the Generate mental state. It also allows me to get more out of my energy when I go back over the writing, in another mental state.

When Paul McCartney was working on the unnamed song that would become "Yesterday," he had a trick that effectively helped him stay in the right mental state. Remember from the previous chapter that as he was playing the melody for friends, McCartney still didn't have lyrics for his song. So, he used placeholder lyrics. The song wasn't called "Yesterday." It was called "Scrambled Eggs." The lyrics were so nonsensical, there was no way he was going to actually use them. Don't believe me? The first verse started, "Scrambled eggs, oh my baby how I love your legs."

THROUGH TRIAL and error, I developed my grab bag of rituals for various types of work. I adjusted my environment, changed my tools, or even changed what I drank, according to the mental state I wanted to achieve.

The gyokuro green tea I drank during my evening Research or Explore sessions was imported directly from a grower in Japan. I specifically selected this variety of tea for the state of relaxed focus it encouraged. Gyokuro leaves are shaded at a specific point in their growth cycle. This gives the tea its distinct aroma and sweet flavor, but it also boosts the leaves' theanine content. I then supplemented the tea with additional theanine.

Theanine is an amino acid – scarce in a regular diet – that synergizes with caffeine. When used with caffeine, theanine promotes a state of relaxed focus. It takes the "edge" off caffeine. Which is important, because caffeine can cause anxiety. So, a cup of gyokuro, with some extra theanine thrown in, helped trigger the focus I needed for my night-time research sessions.

The glass of wine I drank in the early evening at the Whole Foods wine bar also promoted relaxation. After a long day in the Polish or Research mental state, the alcohol helped me let loose for a generation session. Obviously, you have to use caution with alcohol. My session would have been counterproductive if I had drunk a whole bottle.

TOOLS FOR THOUGHT: THE SLIPPY & THE GRIPPY

I also chose my tools according to the mental state I was trying to promote. Some tools are "grippy," meaning they make it easy to stay on task – you can write with a pen and paper without distraction. Other tools are "slippy," meaning they make it easy to get off task – you can write faster on a computer than you can with pen and paper, but it's easy to get distracted. The downside of grippy tools is: The grippier the tool, the less likely what you produce with that tool will become a finished product. The upside of slippy tools is that if you can manage to stay on task with a slippy tool, you'll produce your finished product faster than with a grippy tool.

Every tool you use has a symbiotic relationship with your abilities while using that tool. A chimp fishing for ants with a stick can't use her hand for another purpose while holding that stick. Whatever tool you use will make it easier to do some things, while making it harder to do other things.

For example, a laptop is a very slippy tool for a writer. You can write prose very quickly, and you can quickly navigate between documents and applications. You can do research, stitch together writing from various places, or draw simple diagrams.

But, because the laptop is so slippy, you can easily get distracted. You can get stuck surfing the web, or fiddling around on social media. With a slippy tool, you can quickly turn any thought into a finished product, but you can just as easily turn any thought into a path to distraction.

By contrast, a notebook and pen is a very grippy tool for writing. Once you start writing in a notebook, there's no way for the notebook to distract you. There are no notifications, and you can't use it to look anything up. You can do lots of writing in a notebook, but you're unlikely to use that writing as a final product. It's best to be in the Explore mental state when writing in a notebook. You're trying out ideas, but those ideas won't really come to fruition until you revisit them in a Generate mental state – likely with a slippier tool.

If a tool is designed for a specific outcome, it can hit a sweet spot between slippy and grippy. The portable word processor I use for my morning writing habit is a good example. The AlphaSmart NEO is simply a keyboard with a cheap one-color LCD screen – the kind you would find on an old-school graphing calculator.

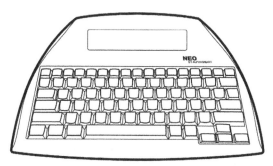

The AlphaSmart is designed for writing, and writing only. It has a full keyboard. But, the AlphaSmart has no internet capability, so there's no chance you'll end up surfing the web. You can write so easily on the AlphaSmart, it feels like a slippy tool. But since that's all you can do, it's also quite grippy.

The AlphaSmart is a good tool for staying within a mental state. You can only view about four lines of type on the screen at a time, which makes it difficult to do any editing. Even if you wanted to switch into the Polish mental state, you would have a hard time. So, you keep writing.

I mostly use the AlphaSmart for exploratory writing sessions – where the writing is more about exercising the ideas in my mind, and trusting that they'll resurface later. However, if I happen to capture some writing I don't want to lose, I can transfer that writing to my laptop via a USB cable.

The USB cable transfer is one of many inconvenient things about the AlphaSmart, and that's the point. Sometimes you want a tool that *can't* do certain things, so you can focus more deeply on the things you *can* do. You can't make a colorful oil painting with a pencil, but the limitations of a pencil reduce the number of factors you can worry about. You can't worry about color, and you can't worry about the character of brushstrokes on the completed canvas. A pencil will focus your mind on the shapes you're drawing and the overall arrangement of your composition. It's no wonder that for years before Vincent van Gogh used color in groundbreaking ways, he worked strictly in black and white. He

THE SEVEN MENTAL STATES OF CREATIVE WORK 125

mastered one aspect of painting before mastering another. Georgia O'Keeffe also focused on drawing in black and white early in her artistic journey, ignoring the color she had previously "gone mad" about.

Writers don't have to buy a portable word processor to help them stay in the right mental state. You can enhance an existing tool so it encourages a mental state. I now do much of my writing on an external keyboard attached to my tablet. Switching applications on a tablet is more cumbersome than on a laptop. I'm unlikely to get stuck surfing the web, but it's also less convenient to look up reference material. It keeps me in the Generate mental state.

You can also purposefully limit the capabilities of a tool. My tablet is less distracting than it might be otherwise because I have rules about what my tablet is for, and what it is not for. For example, I don't allow social media applications on my tablet. I also don't allow notifications. I use it only for a specific set of functions: reading, writing, and video chatting. You don't have to have device-wide rules to make such modifications. For example, some applications allow you to place restrictions on what websites you can visit during certain times of day.

YOU CAN choose and adjust your tools according to the mental state you want to encourage, but you can also change your environment. I later learned that there were scientific explanations for why some settings in my grab bag of rituals were effective for certain types of work.

MAKE THE ROOM WORK FOR YOU

Donald M. Rattner is an architect with a special interest in how our surroundings affect our creative thinking. In his book, *My Creative Space*, Donald draws from the field of environmental psychology to make recommendations on how to enhance creativity by altering your environment – whether that's the amount of space, the colors and shapes that surround you, lighting, or even your body position.

I asked him if he could explain why my visits to the top of a skyscraper put me in the Prioritize mental state. He introduced me to a concept called "construal level theory." Donald says that construal level theory states that "the farther away you perceive an object, an incident, or an event, the more abstract, broad-minded, big-picture, broad-brush-thinking mindset you get into."

Construal level theory also explains why the backroom at Ipsento Coffee was a good place for editing my writing. It was a small space, with a low ceiling. Not only do you think big-picture when you're in an open space, Donald told me you think small-picture when you're in a small space. "Generally the threshold for [ceiling height] for generating ideas would be ten feet or higher. Whereas eight feet and lower you start to become more focused in your thinking, more analytic, more calculating, which of course is the mirror of creative thinking." Plus, the darker lighting turned my laptop screen into a sort of portal for my attention. The narrowing of my attention put me in a Polish mental state.

Donald added that another concept, called "prospect refuge theory," is also consistent with thinking more openly while at the top of a skyscraper. Prospect refuge theory proposes that we're evolutionarily wired to be more comfortable when we can see out into our surroundings. Our ancestors who were able to seek habitats where they could see approaching danger had a better chance of survival. Donald said, "We're not expecting to be attacked in our own homes from behind by a wild animal. And yet our brains, because evolution moves so slowly, haven't caught up to the fact that we're now living in a modern built environment."

A recent study illustrates how prospect refuge theory can make us think bigger and more boldly. It found that stock traders working in the upper floors of a tall building took more risks than stock traders working in the lower floors of the tower.

One way to create your own rituals for getting into the right mental state for the task at hand is to change your environment. According to Donald, to be more creative, look for open spaces, especially with a view. To be more analytical, look for closed spaces. So for the Explore, Generate, Prioritize, and Recharge mental states, go for open spaces. For Research, Polish, and Administrate mental states, go for closed spaces.

Noise level can also affect your ability to think creatively. Intuitively, we think it's best to work in a quiet environment. But when it comes to creativity, studies suggest that a background noise level of about seventy decibels is optimal for idea generation. But it has to be indistinct noise. If you can clearly understand a conversation happening next to you, that can be distracting. This is one of the benefits I've found of living in a country where people don't speak my native language – unless I make it a point to focus on the cafe chatter around me, I understand very little.

Your body position while you're working can also affect your mental state. Donald told me, "sitting is probably the least conducive position to being in a divergent mindset. But standing seems to help us not only in terms of creativity but also productivity as well," which supports the recent standing-desk craze.

Donald adds that "A second position that's good is reclining." Numerous writers and thinkers worked in bed, including René Descartes, Marcel Proust, and Edith Warton. Frida Kahlo began painting seriously while bedridden from a bus accident. Truman Capote proclaimed himself to be "a completely horizontal author," and Michael Chabon writes laid back in an Eames chair – his laptop resting on the kind of overbed table you might see in a hospital.

But you don't have to stay in bed all day. Donald also says, "creativity and locomotion seem to go hand in hand.… Taking walks, exercising, all of these things that get the blood flowing…are almost always positive in terms of creative output."

You can also combine a grippy tool with locomotion. Donald suggests that transforming a wall into a whiteboard or chalkboard can get you into an expansive thinking mode. You can use your whole body while drawing on a wall, which would be good for the Prioritize or Explore mental states. This is what was great about having a big whiteboard on the floor during my nighttime Research and Exploration sessions. Donald says, "If you want to think big, draw big."

It's great if you can change your setting to suit your desired mental state, but you don't need to have complete control over your environment. If you can't escape from your office to your favorite cafe, you might be able to grab a conference room, or find a place away from your desk to sit or stand – depending upon the mental state you want to encourage.

You can also make tweaks to your space without moving at all. When I first started on my own, I had a tiny bedroom at the end of a shotgun house in San Francisco. There were plenty of cafes at my doorstep, but I was still working after they were closed, and there were only a few feet separating my bed from my desk. I didn't want to condition myself to think about work while in bed, and I didn't want to condition myself to think about sleep while at my desk.

So I designed a series of cues to switch mental states on command. When it was time to work, I deployed a shoji screen – one of those collapsible room dividers with translucent panels. I clipped a lamp onto it to deflect light in a certain way, steeped a cup of chamomile tea, and started playing a particular album. Once everything was in place, I quickly sank into a focused state. When I was done working, I changed the lighting and hid my desk with the shoji screen. It was just enough of a change in environment to separate sleep and work.

WHILE THERE is plenty of scientific research about conditions that encourage certain mental states, use this information only as a guideline. What works for one type of thinking under experimental conditions may not work for the exact type of thinking you're trying to do in the real world.

My habit of facing a blank wall in the morning, for example, runs counter to the notion that open spaces lead to better creative thinking. My desk is in a little cove, I'm vulnerable to a rear attack from saber-toothed tigers, and I'm even wearing earplugs to drown out any background noise. Yes, I am writing and trying to think creatively, but I'm in a more strict Generate mental state. I'm trying to actually get work done. While I'm groggy and thus prone to having insights, I'm also very distractible. If I'm distractible, it makes it difficult to execute on ideas. I shape my environment to rein in the less desirable aspects of my mental state.

YOUR OWN PERSONAL PLACEBO

Even if experimental findings are helpful, ultimately, nearly any set of conditions can trigger the right state. In his book, *The Art of Learning,* chess champion and performance coach Josh Waitzkin describes how he helped an executive get into the right mental state for meetings. The executive said he most felt in "flow," when he was playing catch with his son. He wished he could feel that same way in his meetings – instead, he felt distracted.

Josh designed a series of cues for this executive to follow to trigger the right mental state for his meetings. Josh conditioned him to associate other cues with that flow state. He told the executive to play catch with his son every day. But leading up to playing catch with his son, he was to follow a routine. He ate a light snack, meditated, followed a stretching routine, then played catch with his son. While playing catch with his son, he listened to a Bob Dylan song.

He followed this routine for a while, then tried performing it right before a meeting. It helped him get into the right state. Gradually, he compressed the routine, removing pieces, until he didn't need to do any of it to get into the right state for a meeting. He could merely *think* of the Bob Dylan song, and he would be ready.

While playing catch triggered a flow state in the executive, not everyone would feel the same way. It was his personal experience and relationship with his son that made playing catch an effective cue. And it was through repeatedly chaining that cue with other cues that he was able to design a routine that got him into the desired state.

Twyla Tharp has a stretching and weight-training routine she does every morning. But to her, the routine doesn't begin at the gym. The routine begins when she stumbles out of bed at 5:30 a.m., puts on her clothes, and hails a cab. She knows that if she can get herself into that cab, she won't be tempted to skip a workout.

Creativity coach Mark McGuinness has a Japanese *Star Wars* mug at his desk. He knows that when he fills that mug with coffee and places it on his desk, it will put him in a mental state for writing.

It's like novelist Nicholson Baker said, "you could say to yourself, 'From now on, I'm only going to write on the back porch in flip flops starting at four o'clock in the afternoon.'

And if that feels novel and fresh, it will have a placebo effect and it will help you work."

THE RITUALS or routines that get you into the right mental state to do your work could be anything. To start building the right routines, start thinking about mental state. Ask yourself, *What state do I need to be in to do this work?*, and *When was the last time I felt that way?* See if you can reverse engineer your way back into that state by recreating the conditions. Go to the same place, drink the same drink, and perform the same routine. If you can't return to the same setting, see if you can replicate the environment. Was the space expansive, or closed? Was the lighting bright or dim, focused or dispersed? Was it noisy, or quiet?

Once you've recreated the right mental state, try to stay within that state, without switching to others. Pay close attention to the task at hand. Do you notice that some aspects of the task cause you to shift out of the mental state? Save those parts for another time. Remember that generation is different from exploration, that exploration is different from research, and that polishing your work too early can waste valuable creative energy. Remember that you'll be more focused if you set aside separate time to think about priorities, that administrative details don't deserve your best creative energy, and that you need to take time to recharge, so you can replenish that creative energy.

Keep your mental state in mind when you choose your tools, and the level of development of your ideas. If you're still trying to think as creatively as possible, choose a grippy tool that won't tempt you with distractions. If it's time to execute, choose a slippy tool. For best results, modify that slippy tool to be grippy only for the task at hand.

When you create according to mental state, a new world will open up. You'll have more energy to create things, and more confidence in your ability to follow through. Your creative energy will no longer be wasted on haphazardly switching mental states.

But you can do even more to make the most of your mental energy. You can go beyond adjusting your environment and your tools. Yes, your work progresses through the Four Stages of Creativity more smoothly when you work according to mental state. But when you master how mental states cycle throughout time, you truly have a well-oiled creative machine.

CHAPTER 5

CREATIVE CYCLES

*A great inequality is observable in the vigor of
the mind at different periods of the day.*

—THOMAS JEFFERSON

"CAN I talk to you for a second?" Jonathan said. I stopped in the doorway. "Are you sure about this?" he continued. "This seems kind of rash. You've been unemployed for a year, you've been working on your business until 4 a.m. every night, and it's not going so well. I'm not sure you're making the right decision."

My roommate was right to be concerned. My behavior was unusual. I had spent the past year working twelve- and sixteen-hour days, and not making a dime. Meanwhile, startups were recruiting me. I had design and coding skills, I lived in San Francisco, and it was 2008. I had incredible opportunities in front of me, but I wasn't interested in them. Instead, without warning, I announced that I was moving. "Who moves from San Francisco to Chicago?" Jonathan said. "It's supposed to be the other way around."

But there was a method to this madness. I wanted to produce an effect. I was working with and against the forces around me to achieve that effect. I was employing what I would later call Creative Cycles.

Two years later, my plan bore fruit. It came to me on a

mild July day, as I was sitting at a picnic table on the porch of Noble Tree Coffee. *Is this real?* I asked myself. I did a quick search on the web. Nothing. I checked to see if the website domain I wanted was available. It was. My breath quickened. My heart pounded. My hands shook. I said to myself, *This is it*. It was my Big Idea.

It had started with a feeling. A feeling that I had more thoughts than I could hold in my brain. I sensed that something in there was worthwhile. I had an inkling that if I gave myself the time and the space to explore those thoughts, I would find something unique. My Big Idea.

To begin, I cashed out a good portion of my retirement account. For the next year, I turned down every freelance gig and every job offer. I even turned away a Facebook recruiter – an opportunity that may have been worth millions. I didn't want any distractions. I needed to sort through what was in my mind.

Eventually, that desire for space and quiet – and cheaper rent – drove me out of San Francisco. I needed to isolate myself from whatever the hot new trend was in startups and tech. None of it would help me find what I was looking for.

Jonathan was right. For much of that first year of working on my own in San Francisco, I was up until 4 a.m. But, I was still getting plenty of sleep. I had simply shifted my schedule. From midnight to 4 a.m., I did a solid block of focused work. When I did lose focus, there were no distractions for me to escape to. I'd hit refresh on my email inbox or my social media accounts, and there were no updates – aside from the occasional tweet from someone on the other side of the globe. In the middle of the night, everyone was asleep – even in Silicon Valley.

At 4 a.m., I'd transform my tiny room from a place for working into a place for sleeping: Turn off the lamp, tuck my chair under my desk, and wrap the shoji screen around the desk. Go to bed, and sleep until noon. Tomorrow, I'd work from one cafe after another until they were all closed. Then I'd transform my bedroom back into an office to do it all again.

I didn't have a name for it at the time, but I was building a Creative Cycle. A Creative Cycle is a repeatable progression of focus and release. You're intentionally doing the Preparation, and providing the Incubation. By repeating this pattern, you eventually achieve Illumination. Then, you can do the Verification necessary to bring your work into the world.

You can build more effective Creative Cycles if you pay attention to the rhythms around you. You'll find these rhythms in the natural world, such as sunrises and sunsets, and the change of seasons. You'll also find these rhythms in cultural cues, such as our designations of days, weeks, and months – and in our rituals around eating, sleeping, or celebrating holidays. Finally, you'll find these rhythms in your own energy fluctuations. There will be times when your energy lends itself to being creative, and other times when your energy lends itself to being analytical.

When you master Creative Cycles, you harness the energy provided by these rhythms. You propel your creative projects forward, with each action creating potential energy for other actions. You work like a perpetual creativity machine.

When I shifted my schedule so that I worked through the middle of the night, I created a cycle that harnessed power from the rhythms of cultural cues. When everyone was asleep, I could get more work done. When everyone was awake – sending distracting emails and messages, and posting social media updates – I was sleeping.

When I moved from San Francisco to Chicago, I created a different Creative Cycle. This time, I harnessed the power of the dramatic change of seasons.

"I know it's strange," I told Jonathan. "I never thought I'd say this, but: I miss winter."

COASTING WITH CYCLES

I hated winter with a passion. I still do. When I first moved to California, I smugly posted a screenshot of the six-day forecast on my blog, for my friends in Nebraska to see. So I surprised even myself when I started to miss winter.

I didn't miss scraping ice and snow off my car in the darkness before work. I didn't miss owning an entire wardrobe I couldn't wear half the year. I didn't miss scrubbing a dried sludge of salt and sand and melted snow out of my entryway carpet.

The one thing I did miss was the feeling of having no choice. I missed those days when I said to myself, *Well, it's below zero, there's six inches of snow on the ground, it's falling so fiercely you can't see three feet in front of yourself, and it's been dark since 4 p.m. I guess I'm staying in.* I didn't stay in to watch TV, play video games, or eat junk food. I read books and I worked on projects. I learned and explored.

So when I decided to move to Chicago, I wanted to go back to having no choice but to stay in and create. I wanted an extremely long cycle in the Explore mental state. As winter gave way to summer and back again, my Big Idea went from the Preparation stage, to the Incubation stage, and right back again, over and over. The time between starting on my own and the day I had the idea for my first book on the porch of Noble Tree Coffee spanned three years.

Creative Cycles don't have to take three years, and whatever longer cycles you use, smaller cycles feed them. It's like how the tiny gears on a clock move the larger gears. Even when I was on this three-year cycle, other smaller cycles were happening. Each season in Chicago helped guide my project through the Four Stages of Creativity.

Summer in Chicago is like a manic episode. Everyone tries to spend as much time as possible outside. You spend your day in big, expansive spaces. You move around, ride your bike, eat at rooftop restaurants, or go to concerts and street festivals. It's a good time for having Big Ideas.

By contrast, in the winter, you're in enclosed spaces. It's dark. The conditions are right for time spent in the Explore, Research, Generate, and Polish mental states. It's a good time for the Preparation or Verification stages of a big project.

The winter in Chicago is so oppressive, by the time summer comes, you need a break. You spend as much of the summer as possible in the Recharge mental state. Your big projects are in the Incubation stage. Illumination can happen at any moment. It's not a coincidence that the idea for my first book came to me while sitting outside on a beautiful summer day, after two long winters of exploration.

Think of Creative Cycles the way you would think of pedaling a bicycle uphill in high gear. If you try to apply the same amount of force to each pedal at all times, you will waste energy and burn yourself out. It's on the downstrokes of each pedal when you should be applying the most force. That's when your energy translates to forward motion. You could call that area where the pedal has just passed over the apex of its path the "sweet spot." When a pedal hits the sweet spot, you stand up on the pedals and use the laws of physics to get more power. You shift your weight from side to side, so that gravity applies your bodyweight to each pedal just as each pedal hits the sweet spot.

Finding my Creative Sweet Spot was an important part of building my own Creative Cycles. I found that there was a time of day when I was better-suited to be in a Generate mental state. But I eventually found that there was a Creative Sweet Spot not only within my day, but within many other cycles: Within a given week, month, even year, or within even longer cycles, there are times when I can generate new ideas more easily. Not only that, but there are sweet spots for each of the Seven Mental States of Creative Work.

QUIT YOUR DAILY ROUTINE. START YOUR WEEKLY ROUTINE.

You probably have a daily routine. Get up, eat breakfast,

Sample Creative Cycles, by time of day, day of week, or
season of year – showing how each stage of each cycle could
match up with the Four Stages of Creativity.

shower, go to work, check email, plan your day, etc. You repeat that routine every day, and you follow a different routine on the weekends. But if you look closely, many of us are already following routines that go beyond the daily routine, and are actually weekly routines. We get a case of "the Mondays." By Wednesday's "hump day" we're wishing we could say "Thank God It's Friday."

There are subtle changes in behavior that come along with these rhythms. For example, online marketers know Tuesday is a hot day to debut anything – whether a blog post, a new book, or an album. There's simply way more activity on the internet on Tuesdays. Why is that? Maybe it's because when everyone got to work on Monday, they had to catch up with what happened over the weekend. They weren't reading articles, and they only read the most important emails. Now that it's Tuesday, they feel like they deserve a little break. So, they spend more time on social media, or they pay more attention to a marketing email that hits their inbox.

By contrast, I used to run an online dating blog, and Sundays were always our biggest day. Single young professionals don't have as much time and attention for looking for dates throughout the week. Friday and Saturday nights, they go out. By Sunday, they have some free time, don't have other plans, and maybe after yet another boring night at the bars they feel more motivated to find someone special.

The routines we follow each day are shaped by cues all around us. The sun rises and sets, most of the professional world follows a nine-to-five schedule, and we tend to have meals at certain intervals during the day. As Daniel Pink described in *When: The Scientific Secrets of Perfect Timing*, we're wired with biological clocks that influence when we're alert and when we're tired, as well as our mood and many other factors.

But many of these cues work beyond the daily cycle. One of the most reliable cycles is the weekly cycle. By following a weekly cycle, you can deepen your focus and reduce procrastination. So, instead of having a daily routine, have a weekly routine.

I first learned about organizing according to a weekly routine from productivity consultant Ari Meisel. He has his entire week organized by what category of activities he does, at what time. If he has paperwork to take care of, for example, he knows he'll save it for Friday at 10 a.m.

Ari helped me realize there are a number of benefits to having designated days of week and times of day for doing certain tasks. One is that you save mental energy by single-tasking, instead of multitasking. He said, "In an hour we don't want to be doing a phone call, then two minutes later getting on Excel and trying to work on something, then answering a Facebook notification, then getting back on the phone and going to get a cup of coffee, and then talking to a coworker. By the end of the hour you've done sixty things but you've actually not gotten anything done."

When you randomly switch from one activity to another, your energy leaks. When you switch gears on a motor, energy is wasted in continuing to move those gears when they are no longer coupled with one another. If you're doing that all the time, little of your energy is going toward traction. As Nir

Eyal says in his book, *Indistractable*, the opposite of traction is dis-traction.

The other benefit of having designated times to do certain types of tasks is that it focuses your energy on the task at hand. Not only are you preventing energy leaks by not switching rapidly from one task to another, but you're also more focused in the moment. "Science shows us that our brains work better in sprints than they do in marathons," said Meisel.

When I first tried to organize my tasks by time of week, it was a struggle. Some tasks were time-sensitive, and didn't feel like they could wait. With practice, I was eventually able to put off tasks that could wait until another time.

If my accountant sent me an email on a Monday, asking me to review financial statements, my natural reaction was to stop what I was doing and review the financial statements. As I tried to put it off to another time, I made excuses to myself about why it couldn't wait. I didn't want to seem unresponsive, and I convinced myself it was urgent. It turned out nothing bad happened if I intentionally put off a task, and if I was worried about seeming unresponsive, I could send a quick email telling the other person when I would get it done.

Designating certain times to do certain work had a number of unexpected benefits. First, deciding when I would do a task reduced procrastination. That's right: What was essentially intentional procrastination, actually served to reduce procrastination. I had made a mental and verbal commitment, and I wanted to stay consistent with that commitment. This was a stark contrast from my usual reaction to an email, which was to stare at my screen for several minutes, intending to review the financial statements, while thinking about the other things I wanted or needed to do. By knowing I would review my financial statements later, I could get back to the work I was doing before the email appeared in my inbox.

The second benefit was that deciding when I would do a task made me more organized, and motivated me to prevent crises. When a task did come up that I couldn't put off, I asked myself, *How did this task become urgent?* After experiencing the joys of being focused in the moment, I wanted to maximize those moments. I created systems that prevented crises, and that made my business bulletproof when inevitable crises did arise. (I'll tell you more about those systems in the next chapter.)

The third and most profound benefit of deciding ahead of time when to do certain tasks was that I started to achieve a rhythm that made better use of my creative energy. At first, my choices of when to do a task were arbitrary. But I eventually altered those choices to make better use of my energy, based upon fluctuations in energy I noticed throughout my week.

By now it was clear I didn't want to review financial statements on a Monday. So, when was the best time to review financial statements? Matching my tasks with fluctuations in my energy – and thus with the ideal mental state – eventually made the answer clear.

On Mondays, I have fresh creative energy from a

weekend away from work. I've been through a period of Incubation, and now I'm ready for moments of Illumination. Why would I waste my best creative energy on financial statements? I want to be in the Generate mental state, not the Administrate mental state. Tuesdays are no good either. I've shaken off the cobwebs from the weekend, and I've hit my stride. I'm ready to explore the loose ends that showed up in my Monday Generate session. My projects are ready for some more Preparation, done either in the Explore or Research mental states.

While I was working on Timeful, I got further practice deciding ahead of time when to do tasks. What I learned from that practice later combined with my mental state rhythms to make even better use of my creative energy, essentially transforming myself into a perpetual creativity machine.

WHAT I LEARNED ABOUT PRODUCTIVITY WHILE WORKING ON GOOGLE CALENDAR

Think about how most of us use to-do lists. We have our list of things we need to do, but we don't know when we'll do them, or how long those items will take. Our proverbial eyes are bigger than our calendars.

The Timeful team came up with a brilliant feature in which you didn't simply make to-do list items. You could also estimate the time it would take to complete each of those to-do list items, then you could drag the items onto your calendar. The result was to-do items on a timeline, along with all the other events on your calendar. It would quickly become obvious that you didn't actually have time to do everything on your to-do list. As a design advisor, I needed to commit myself to using this feature, and in the process I learned a lot about making good use of my time.

The first thing I learned was that I was bad at estimating how long tasks would take. It turns out we are all bad at estimating how long things will take. Daniel Kahneman and Amos Tversky coined this "the planning fallacy." To see it in action, simply make a list of tasks you'd like to get done within an hour, then try to complete those tasks within the hour. It will be an eye-opening experience.

Usually, the actual time it takes to complete the tasks you've planned will be much longer than what you've estimated. This can be frustrating, but it's also a learning opportunity. Stop and think back to everything that happened over the past hour. Why did you miss your estimate?

I did this exercise, of estimating the time tasks would take, over and over while adding to-do items to my Timeful calendar. I usually missed my estimates for one of three reasons: I was unprepared for the task, I got interrupted, or I was simply overly-optimistic.

When I was unprepared for the task, there was something I needed in order to do the task – which I didn't have. If I needed to write a draft of an article, for example, I was unprepared when I didn't have any research done to help me write that article. This was often an error in identifying the "next action," – as David Allen calls it in *Getting Things Done*. With creative projects, it showed a lack of respect for the Four Stages of Creativity. I didn't have any Preparation, nor

Incubation, and I was foolishly expecting Illumination.

When I got interrupted, the source of that interruption was internal, external, or a combination of both. When I had an internal interruption, a thought came to my mind that got me off task. Maybe I suddenly wondered what year Snoop Dogg was born and couldn't resist looking it up on Wikipedia (1971). When I had an external interruption, some stimulus outside of me drove me off task. Maybe my phone buzzed with a message. Even if I kept my phone on silent and in another room, the task itself would sometimes drive me to an external interruption. For example, a web portal I was signing into would require me to enter a string of digits from my phone, for security purposes. As I'd grab my phone, I'd notice a text message from a friend. I'd then attend to the text message, and get off task.

When I practiced estimating and sticking to times, I found that I got better at staying on task, no matter what the source of interruption. Because I was watching the clock closely, I remembered to mentally bookmark whatever I was doing at the moment of interruption. I was then able to get the interruption out of the way and return to my task.

Other times, I was simply overly-optimistic about my ability to complete the task in my estimated time. Few of us truly think about how long something will take us. We all know that when our friend texts to tell us they'll arrive at the restaurant in five minutes that they'll actually walk through the door in about fifteen minutes. Yet when *we're* running late, we make the same mistake.

We're bad at estimating how long it will take for us to

complete tasks because we get very little practice at it. This was what was so powerful about putting to-do items on a calendar timeline. Most of us simply have a to-do list, but we don't bother thinking about when we'll do the items on the list. Do we even have the time?

My practice of dragging to-do items onto a calendar timeline didn't last forever. When Google bought Timeful, they incorporated some features into Calendar, but they have yet to implement to-do items on a calendar.

That's too bad for lots of people, but it turns out I no longer need the feature. A year of practice in estimating the time tasks took changed the way I saw time forever. My experience throughout my day shifted from being an amorphous blur of half-baked intentions that rarely became real, into a somewhat coherent and lucid progression.

Even if you can't use Timeful or Google Calendar to place your to-do items onto your schedule, you can still experience what happens when you start to estimate how long your tasks will take. You can simply create events on your calendar for each task.

In any case, don't let not having the perfect tool stop you from trying this powerful exercise. You can draw a timeline on paper the next time you sit down to do some work. Even doing this one time will change the way you see how you use your time.

Depending upon the level of creativity required for the task, be careful not to get too focused on "clock-time." Remember from Chapter 2 that event-time is better suited for having insights. Practice estimating time and you'll be better at using your time – but when creativity matters, sticking to too strict a schedule will backfire.

Working on Timeful not only taught me a lot about estimating the time tasks take, but it also helped bring clarity to the way my mental states shift throughout the week. Another key feature of Timeful was that it suggested times to do tasks that you hadn't yet put on your calendar. The task would appear on your calendar, and you could accept or reject the proposed time.

It was a brilliant feature, because it's easy to say you're going to write three times a week, but it's much harder to make the commitment of choosing a time to do so. When the team introduced this suggestions feature, I had already begun to organize my tasks according to the best time in the week in which to do those tasks, and I had already begun to choose those times according to the ebb and flow of my mental states. Now that I had begun to organize my week according to mental state I noticed that, early on, the suggestions Timeful made felt off. Yes, you could designate working hours during which tasks would be assigned, and the algorithms knew better than to put tasks in the middle of the night, when you were sleeping, but I also found that the times it was suggesting to do certain tasks were the wrong times, given my fluctuations in mental state.

MENTAL STATES THROUGHOUT THE WEEK

By this point, I had become so accustomed to organizing my tasks by the flow of the week, I was surprised that my observation wasn't obvious to the design team. I said, "The app is suggesting that I write this blog post at 2 p.m. At 2 p.m., there's no chance of me getting any writing done. At 2 p.m., I'm tired from working all morning. I'm ready for a nap, before rebounding in the afternoon. But in the late afternoon I'll be more alert. That would be a better time not for writing the blog post, but for editing it. I need to write first thing in the morning, before the rest of my day gets in the way." The Timeful team then began considering energy fluctuations in their algorithms.

(This is one feature, by the way, that did make it into Google Calendar after Google bought Timeful. It's a feature called "Goals." You tell the mobile app what you'd like to get done, and how often, and it uses patterns in your schedule to suggest the right times to do it.)

Through trial and error, I got more organized about planning my week according to mental state. The rhythm I settled on was a natural extension of the ebb and flow of my own creative energy, and how those energy fluctuations matched up with the cultural cue of the standard work week.

A graph of my creative energy throughout a day looks like this:

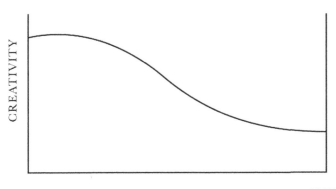

WAKE   SLEEP

My creative energy is highest in the morning, just after waking up. It then wanes throughout the day. Thus, my Creative Sweet Spot is in the mornings.

But my creative energy also fluctuates throughout the week. A graph of my creative energy throughout the week looks like this:

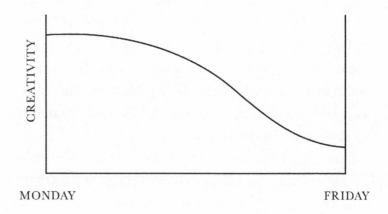

My creative energy is highest toward the beginning of the week. It drops sharply in the middle of the week, and by the end of the week, my creative energy is tapped out, and needs replenishing.

Since creative output is such a high priority for me, it's a high priority for me to take advantage of my very best creative energy. Monday mornings are when the high creative energy of early in the week and the high creative energy of early in the day intersect. So, Monday mornings are my most important Creative Sweet Spot.

The Four Stages of Creativity also influence how best to allocate my creative energy throughout the week. For larger projects, Monday mornings are good for the Illumination stage, because Mondays come after the weekend – which is a period of Incubation.

Throughout the week, as I work on one creative problem, it often serves as Preparation for other creative problems. For example, writing one chapter of a book prepares me to write another chapter in that same book. Loose ends introduced in one chapter call for tying together those loose ends in the next chapter.

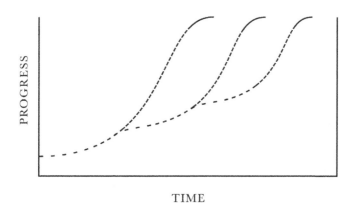

TIME

Additionally, once I have experienced Illumination and generated work, I need to conduct Verification on that work. I need to spend some time in the Polish mental state, which I do on afternoons, especially toward the end of the week.

The nature of creative work and the nature of my creative energy eventually led to predictable patterns in my mental state throughout the week. Early mornings and early in the week were better for the Generate mental state. As the week wore on and as mornings turned into afternoons, I was spending more time in the Research and Polish mental states, revising the work I had created earlier. I took advantage of my mind's "clean slate" on Monday afternoons by spending time in the Explore mental state, which served as Preparation for new ideas. I also spent time in the Explore mental state later in the week, such as Thursday afternoons. This was an opportunity to think about loose ends that had sprung up during the week.

By this process of elimination, it finally became clear when was the right time to review financial statements: Friday afternoons. By Friday afternoon I have already used my best creative energy to do my most important work. Saving this non-critical task for later in the week keeps the task from interfering with my more important tasks, and it allows me to sink more deeply into the right mental state while doing those tasks earlier in the week.

Now, if I get an email from my accountant on a Monday, I use a tool to get that email out of my inbox for the rest of the week. The tool then returns the email to my inbox at the time I designate: Friday afternoon. The task connected to that email is completely out of my mind, until the appropriate time. I'm free to focus more deeply throughout my week.

Through observing how my mental energy fluctuated throughout the week, a predictable rhythm emerged.

Here's how my mental states fluctuate during the course of a typical week:

	MONDAY	TUESDAY	WEDNESDAY	THURSDAY	FRIDAY
MORNING	GENERATE	GENERATE	GENERATE, RESEARCH	GENERATE, RESEARCH	GENERATE, ADMINISTRATE
AFTERNOON	GENERATE, PRIORITIZE, EXPLORE	RESEARCH, POLISH	RESEARCH, POLISH	RESEARCH, EXPLORE	ADMINISTRATE

Earlier in the week, when my creative energy is highest, I spend more time in the Generate mental state. As the week wears on, I spend more time in the Polish mental state. By Friday, I can get to the pesky details that I put off earlier in the week. My best creative energy is tapped out, and I can spend some time in the Administrate mental state.

THE POWERFUL RULE

If you follow a weekly routine such as this, you're bound to end up with "rules" about certain days. These rules are a natural byproduct of prioritizing how you use your energy, but as we saw in Chapter 2 with the First-Hour Rule, rules are a powerful tool. Rules help you work more efficiently.

For example, one of my rules is: I don't have meetings on Mondays or Tuesdays. I'm generally able to stick to this rule. If an incredibly important meeting comes up that helps me meet a high priority, I will make an exception. But I do that very rarely.

This rule has the benefits I talked about earlier: It keeps me from leaking energy by switching tasks, and it helps deepen my focus throughout the day. But it has a third benefit, which is that it means I don't have to watch the clock. It keeps me out of clock-time and lets me stay in event-time. On Mondays and Tuesdays, I don't have to worry about whether I need to wrap something up so I can get ready for a meeting. This is extremely valuable for creative work. It means that if I want to go down a mental rabbit hole and get completely immersed in a project, I can do that – as long as it's Monday or Tuesday. Keeping my schedule meeting-free helps me make the best possible use of my week's best creative energy.

As a natural byproduct of this rule, if I do have a meeting, it will be later in the week. I try to conduct most podcast interviews on Thursdays. Also, since mornings are my Creative Sweet Spot, that leaves afternoons for meetings. So, those Thursday podcast interviews tend to be at the intersection of late in the week and late in the day – on Thursday afternoons.

The one time that I have a regular meeting in the morning is during my bi-weekly meeting with my mastermind partner. I do have those meetings mid-mornings because that's the most mutually-agreeable time for both of us, and those meetings are valuable enough to be worth the compromise. But I'm still able to get a writing session in before that meeting. The meeting is on a Friday, and I only have so much juice left, so I can't accomplish as much writing as I could on a Monday or Tuesday, anyway. I've been in the weeds of my work for two weeks, and am ready to get some input from someone else.

PREFRONTAL MONDAY

I alter my weekly rhythm as priorities shift within my business. For example, I occasionally have what I call a "Prefrontal Monday." "Prefrontal" refers to the prefrontal cortex – that "spoilsport" area of the brain that is responsible for urge suppression, planning, and long-term thinking. The prefrontal cortex is small, but it's incredibly energy hungry.

So, I'm sure to set aside time specifically for planning, especially if I am in between major projects.

If I need to spend a lot of energy in the Prioritize mental state, there's no better day than Monday. I've disconnected from my work over the weekend. Any bad ideas I was fixated on on Friday, I have forgotten about by Monday. Additionally, I have made it a point to rest – to spend some time in the Recharge mental state – over the weekend. So, of all days in the work week, on Mondays I have the freshest possible energy, and I have the clearest possible picture of what's important in my business.

It's no mistake that when Steve Jobs was CEO of Apple, he spent his Monday mornings in a long meeting with his executive team. From Walter Isaacson's biography of Jobs:

> The key venue for freewheeling discourse was the Monday morning executive team gathering, which started at 9 and went for three or four hours. The focus was always on the future: What should each product do next? What new things should be developed? Jobs used the meeting to enforce a sense of shared mission at Apple. This served to centralize control, which made the company seem as tightly integrated as a good Apple product, and prevented the struggles between divisions that plagued decentralized companies.

As it happens, the prefrontal cortex is known as "the executive of the brain." Jobs sought to centralize control with these executive meetings in order to use Apple's resources wisely. Jobs once said "I'm actually as proud of many of the things we haven't done as the things we have done." Choosing what you won't do, so you can focus on what you will do, is the job of an executive, and it's also the job of the prefrontal cortex.

PRIORITIZE PRIORITIZATION
WITH THE WEEKLY REVIEW

Mondays are a good time to spend in the Prioritize mental state, but so are Sundays. Many people who follow David Allen's *Getting Things Done* methodology spend a block of time in the Prioritize mental state on Sundays. It's called the "weekly review," and it's critical to following a weekly creative cycle. During your weekly review, you review everything you have going on and set your priorities.

I don't spend every Monday in the Prioritize mental state, but I never skip a weekly review. The main distinction between my Sunday weekly review and a Prefrontal Monday is that Prefrontal Mondays are strictly for evaluating my priorities in my business. My Sunday weekly review, however, is mostly concerned with my general schedule and life.

Here's the checklist of items I follow for my weekly review:

» Process inboxes
» Review calendar
» Make dinner invitations
» Confirm appointments
» Review upcoming
» Plan workout
» Do @thisweek items
» Cut vegetables
» Organize supplements

I won't go into great detail on each of those items, but generally, I process everything I've captured throughout the week and make sure I have everything set up for the coming week. The goal is to make it easy to be in the moment throughout the week.

I spend time dedicated to the Prioritize mental state, and I make sure I don't have to switch to the Prioritize mental state throughout the week.

For example, notice that one of my items is to review my calendar. Most people simply wake up in the morning and review their calendars. This is a waste of mental energy. You have to switch to the Prioritize mental state when you review your calendar: Am I ready for this meeting? Does Jessie have everything she needs for soccer practice? With my specific rhythms of creative energy, this would be a disaster. My prefrontal cortex is still sleeping after I wake up. That's no good for planning, but it is good for creating. I would rather spend my morning writing, in the Generate mental state.

Whatever you have on your calendar, there are things to consider that most of us don't think about until the last moment. When we think about these things, we have to switch to the Prioritize mental state. The best example is travel plans.

It used to be that if I had a flight at 2 p.m., I made a number of decisions that morning: What time do I want to arrive at the airport? How long will it take me to get there? What time do I have to leave to arrive at that time? What do I need to pack? My entire morning was spent considering these questions, while trying to follow my usual routine of writing, and my usual meal schedule.

Not surprisingly, I learned to associate travel with anxiety. It seemed no matter how early I left for the airport, I felt anxious about everything that could go wrong. Even if everything was fine, I worried it was not. This din of anxiety crept into the hours and even the days leading up to the trip. It even made it hard to write on the morning of my trip.

Now, I ask myself all these questions ahead of time, as I review my calendar during my weekly review. I take the time to make sure I know when I need to wake up, when I need to be done showering, and when I need to head to the airport. I schedule my ride ahead of time. So, now I can have a normal morning writing session. I have outsourced my Prioritize mental state to my weekly review.

To begin reviewing my calendar during my weekly review, I type out my schedule in a bullet-point list. I create bullets for each day of the week, sub-bullets for "day" and "night." Under those sub-bullets, I then type out any events on my calendar.

Here's what a day of my bullet-point calendar might look like:

» Monday
    » Day
       » 5:00 a.m. wake
       » 6:00 a.m. cab to airport (16–26 minute drive)
       » 6:30 a.m. arrive PHX
       » 7:35 a.m. flight to Chicago
       » 1:05 p.m. arrive ORD

» 2:30 p.m. arrive Phil's house
    » Order groceries while in cab
» Night
    » 8 p.m. dinner, Galway Arms
        » Invite Anton, Andy, Julie
    » 10 p.m. dancing, Reverie

That's just one day (albeit a busy one). I type out a list like this for each day in the coming week. I don't type out most routine things, such as my morning writing sessions, showering, or eating lunch at home. However, if I'm working on a new routine, I will type those events into my list.

It may seem redundant to type out what's already on my calendar, but it serves two specific purposes. First, typing out an event activates that event in my mind. As soon as I type an event in my list, I get ideas about things related to the event that I haven't thought of. As sub-bullets of the event, I then type out things I may need to do to prepare for that event. If I'm planning a dinner out Thursday night, I'll type out that I need to make a reservation in one sub-bullet, and I'll brainstorm whom I'd like to invite in another sub-bullet. From there, I can put the tasks in my task management software, or simply do the tasks.

The second purpose of typing out what's already on my calendar is that it saves mental energy throughout the week. Simply thinking about and typing each event on my calendar programs it into my mind. I may not be able to tell you off the top of my head exactly what is on my calendar for the whole week, but, after an exercise like this, I'll certainly know more about my schedule than if I were relying entirely upon looking at my calendar.

Another item on my weekly review checklist that's worth mentioning is to do "@thisweek" items. "@thisweek" is the actual filename of the note in which I do my weekly review, such as my bullet-point calendar review. The "@" is inspired by the *Getting Things Done* concept of there being a context for every action. For example, you can only do certain tasks @home, or @office. @thisweek is a temporal context. These are items that are best done in a given week: this week.

Throughout the week, whenever something comes up that I need to address during my weekly review, I put it in my @thisweek note. If I remember a family member's birthday is coming up, I put a note in @thisweek. If I have a trip coming up that I need to plan for, I put a note in @thisweek. Then, I can feel confident that I'll see my note during my weekly review and take the proper action.

This is key to the success of my weekly routine: Be able to off-load whatever comes to mind, and put it in a place where I know I'll get to it at the right time. It helps me stay in the moment throughout the week and keeps me from using personal tasks to procrastinate on my professional tasks.

The items in my @thisweek note are often ongoing projects with a long time horizon. This allows me to treat these projects just as I would a creative project. Before I get too far into that, I need to stress that one of the key components of Creative Cycles is their power to use one specific stage of the Four Stages of Creativity, to get better ideas with less effort, and less stress. Creative Cycles help you deliberately tap into the power of Incubation.

EMPLOY YOUR PASSIVE GENIUS

Whether your Creative Cycles are working with the rhythms of the world around you, or with the ebb and flow of your creative energy, Incubation is happening. If focused effort is like the stroke of a bicycle pedal, Incubation is like the momentum that lets you keep coasting well after that concentrated effort.

We have all experienced the power of Incubation. You've been stuck on a problem, only to return to it the next day with newfound clarity. We all know that before you make a big decision, you should "sleep on it." It's as if a "Passive Genius" is in our subconscious, working to solve our creative problems while we do something else. Yet few of us use this Passive Genius intentionally in our daily creative work. In a world where we're always focused on progress and results, it's easy to forget that sometimes the best thing we can do to make progress on a project is: nothing at all.

Incubation takes place whether you're doing nothing at all, or you're doing something unrelated to the problem at hand. Information is passing from your short-term memory, into your long-term memory. You're forgetting the weak connections that lead to bad ideas and bolstering the strong connections that lead to good ideas.

When I have my most important Generation session of the week, on Monday morning, I'm reaping the benefits of Incubation. I've disconnected from my work over the weekend, and by the time I return, my Passive Genius has cleared away the weak connections and reinforced the strong connections. The same thing happens, on a smaller level, throughout the rest of my week. I'm working on my most important creative project each morning. The rest of the day, and overnight as I sleep, that project is in Incubation – my Passive Genius is working on it.

On a smaller level still, is a technique that I call the Alternating Incubation Method. With this method, you can complete two projects in parallel, while harnessing the power of Incubation. Let's say, for example, that I need to write two intro scripts for my podcast. I'll begin by writing a rough draft of the first script. I'll then start writing the rough draft for the second script. After that, I'll return to the first script to edit it. Suddenly, the first script is easier to write. It's been incubating while I was writing the draft of the second script. I alternate between the two scripts, until they're both complete.

Before I used the Alternating Incubation Method, I tried to power through each script, one at a time. At some point, I hit a block. That block made it easy to escape into distractions. With the Alternating Incubation Method, however, I avoid blocks. I can be loose and free while writing my first draft, knowing that I'll soon return to it with newfound clarity. By alternating five-minute bursts on the two scripts, I can finish, in only twenty minutes, what might normally take an hour.

Not all projects are good candidates for the Alternating Incubation Method. The amount of Incubation you need in order to achieve a solution depends upon how hard it is to achieve that solution in the first place. If you're working on something you've done many times before, you might not need any breaks at all. If you're working on a project that is unfamiliar, you'll need longer periods of Incubation. When you use Creative Cycles, such as a weekly routine, that Incubation happens naturally over the longer periods away from the problem. So, over longer periods, the Alternating Incubation Method isn't necessary.

Because Incubation naturally happens in between my weekly reviews, I'm able to achieve clarity on big personal projects on which I might otherwise procrastinate. Notice that on my list of things to do during my weekly review is "do @thisweek items." Whenever I think of a big project I want to or need to take on – such as planning a trip, or figuring out how to file my Colombian taxes – I put the item in my @thisweek note.

The item I have in my @thisweek note may say "brainstorm San Francisco trip," for example. Before I regularly did weekly reviews, trip planning was exhausting. I sat down with the intention of planning an entire trip in one sitting and ended up frustrated and indecisive.

Now, I break up my trip planning into a series of weekly reviews. In the first review, I brainstorm potential destinations, dates, and itineraries, looking up flights and lodging options only to get a general idea of budget and logistics. I then revisit my plan every week, until I have everything booked.

Obviously, this calls for planning well in advance. This is

why you see "Review upcoming" on my weekly review items. When I review my calendar in my weekly review, I look ahead several weeks. If I see anything big coming up that I know will require complex planning, I make sure to get an early start.

By employing my Passive Genius to use the power of Incubation intentionally, I get more clarity and a better sense of control over the big items that used to dominate my conscious mind throughout the week. I spend less time working on the projects actively, and – since I've reduced much of the mental heavy lifting – I'm less likely to dread getting started, so I'm less likely to procrastinate.

WHEN THERE'S ONLY "NOW," YOU WON'T PROCRASTINATE

Working according to a weekly cycle – with the help of a weekly review – reduces procrastination in another way. It creates a sense that there is only *now* to do the task at hand. When I started writing my first book, it was easy to escape into procrastination. I had six months in front of me, with only one to-do item: Write a book. Now that I do creative projects according to the Four Stages of Creativity and I organize my week according to my rhythms in mental state, I have much smaller pockets of time, with much smaller tasks to address.

If you have eight hours in the day to work, there's plenty of time to procrastinate. But if you've identified a two-hour block in which you can be several times more productive than any other time of day, it creates a sense of urgency.

Additionally, when you work with Creative Cycles, your

tasks are smaller than they would be otherwise. Instead of "write a book," your to-do item is now "brainstorm 500 words on chapter seven," or "research the life of Ignaz Semmelweis."

Smaller tasks are easier to tackle. Smaller units of time are harder to waste. When you create a sense that there's only *now*, you don't procrastinate.

The rhythms of the world lend themselves to a weekly routine, but when you're working with longer units of time, you can focus even more deeply in a particular mental state. In fact, the ideas behind this book came from a week I spent in the Explore mental state. When I am between projects, I sometimes declare what I call a "Week of Want."

WEEK OF WANT

When we're in the thick of a project, we focus on things we feel we *should* do. The purpose of the Week of Want is to reconnect with the things you *want* to do. When I do a Week of Want, I clear as many obligations from my schedule as possible. I cast away any sense of trying to accomplish anything in particular. I give myself an entire week to pursue the answer to one question: "What do I *want* to do right now?"

Most of us, when we make space for side projects, carve out a couple hours in a day, or a particular day in a week. This is better than not working on a side project at all, but there are special benefits to taking an entire week that's dominated by the Explore mental state. The more time you spend away from goal-directed thinking, the more expansive your thinking gets. You get to ideas hiding way below the surface of your consciousness, that you wouldn't get around to thinking about otherwise.

Additionally, those ideas get more space for Incubation. Instead of incubating only while you work on other things, those ideas from below the surface get to incubate during the course of several nights of sleep, all in a row.

When I asked neuroscientist John Kounios about the benefits of taking an entire week, he said there were two potential ways that could improve creative thinking. For one, doing what you want to do improves your mood, which leads to better ideas. He explained, "You're just not going to think about all these other things that are nipping at you. You put them out of your mind – you do that which you want to do. It gives you pleasure, puts you in a positive mood, and it's something you can sustain over the week – and then it can lead to creative thoughts."

Additionally, taking a whole week allows you to get into a deeper state of creativity. "This insightful state of mind is very fragile, and it doesn't take much to make it go away," John told me. "It's easier to get into an analytical state of mind than it is to get into a creative, insightful, state of mind. So if you can create this whole block of time for a week, it allows you to really sink into that state."

In its early days, Google was famous for having "20% time" for all its engineers. Their engineers got to use up to twenty percent of their time on any side project they thought would benefit Google. Like the philosophy behind the Week of Want, Google's 20% time was designed to prevent goal-directed activity from stifling innovation. Specifically, it was designed to keep reasonable employees from being stifled by unreasonable managers. Former Google CEO Eric Schmidt said, "If an employee is under pressure, and the manager says 'You've gotta work harder! You've gotta give me everything you have!,' that employee can legitimately look that boss in the eye and say, 'I'll give you one-hundred percent of my eighty-percent time." 20% time was a way of keeping executive thinking from interfering with creative thinking.

While he was running Microsoft, Bill Gates took "think weeks," in which he went to a secluded cabin to immerse himself in piles of books and articles and think about the future of the company. A 1995 think week prompted Gates to send to the company a memo called "The Internet Tidal Wave," which prompted Microsoft to create its own web browser.

The Week of Want has been a powerful tool for me. In fact, mind management itself was the product of a Week of Want. Behavioral scientist Dan Ariely happened to read my introductory blog post on the concept, and this is what prompted him to approach me to collaborate on Timeful. When Google bought Timeful, I got a surprise paycheck, all thanks to a Week of Want that I had taken almost four years prior.

The Week of Want is a big block of time dominated by the Explore mental state, but you can get the benefits of staying in a particular mental state for a long period of time, no matter what the mental state. When I invited entrepreneur Laura Roeder to be on my podcast, she gave me two choices: I could interview her during one particular week, or I could interview her during another particular week, exactly one month later. When I did interview her I made sure to ask her about it, and my suspicion was confirmed: Laura has a "podcast week." One week out of each month, she does as many podcast appearances as she can.

CYCLES IN CULTURAL CUES

There are cues from the outside world that encourage Creative Cycles beyond the length of a week. As I mentioned with my move to Chicago, the change of seasons encouraged very long cycles. National holidays can also be a good opportunity to spend some time in a mental state. Author Paul Jarvis takes a month-long break from social media during the winter holidays. He says, "creativity needs space and focus to thrive. It also has zero negative impact on my business."

I used to wait until New Year's Day to think about what I wanted to accomplish with my New Year. Now, I begin thinking about it weeks in advance. I intentionally disconnect from anything that would put me in an analytical state of mind during the last few weeks of the year, so I can go into my New Year with a fresh perspective.

I've noticed informal cultural cues connected to the winter holidays and the New Year, too. The first couple months of the year, it's more difficult to schedule guests for my podcast. People have taken a break, and realigned their priorities, and being on a podcast tends not to rank high on that list. Another interesting behavior I noticed while running an online dating blog is that – besides Sundays being a day of high activity – the day after Christmas is the biggest day in online dating, by far. It kicks off a hot season that lasts until Valentine's Day. My theory is that people have put off dating during the winter holidays, and spending time with family has them thinking about finding a partner (and maybe the nagging questions from relatives really do work).

Aside from cues from the outside world, you can also create your own longer cycles. The software firm Basecamp works on what is essentially an eight week cycle. They break down projects so that they never take longer than six weeks. Then, they take two weeks "off." It's not that they don't do any work during this break. Instead, they take care of the loose ends that get ignored when they're driving toward the goal of finishing a project. Then they get ready to take on their next six-week project. Basecamp co-founder and *It Doesn't Have to Be Crazy at Work* co-author Jason Fried told me, "It's kind of like fasting.... Your body is working hard when you eat, and sometimes if you give it a break and you fast for a day, your body gets a chance to clean itself up."

The length of the cycles you should use depend upon what you're trying to accomplish. When I moved to Chicago, I was trying to create a year-long cycle. I knew the harsh winters would force me into deep concentration, followed by summers of rest and elation.

Medellín has different qualities that lend itself to shorter Creative Cycles. The weather in Medellín is about as predictable as you can get. It's roughly room temperature all year round. In fact, Medellín is known as "the city of the eternal spring."

But it wasn't just the agreeable temperature that made Medellín the perfect place to build a creative routine. Living in North America, I had taken as a given that the length of a day varies wildly throughout the year. In the winter, it's dark by 5 p.m., and in the summer, it's light until 9 p.m. This can be a benefit if you're working on a long cycle, but it wreaks havoc on routine. Besides its effects on your mood, it makes it hard to keep a steady sleep schedule.

If you don't think that's a big deal, consider a study done on residents of two separate towns in the southern United States. Since both towns are at the same latitude, they both have the same day-length. But one town is on one side of a timezone, and the other town is on the other side of the same timezone. This doesn't affect the time that people go to work in either of these towns, but it does affect when the sun sets. In the town where the sun sets about an hour earlier, residents go to bed earlier, and so they get about an hour more sleep. The researchers concluded that this extra hour of sleep amounted to a 4.5% increase in wages. They said "A one-hour increase in average daily sleep raises productivity by more than a one-year increase in education."

It took me a while to realize this benefit of building my routine in Medellín: The sun rises and sets at roughly the same time, all year long. Since Medellín is so close to the equator, there's little fluctuation in day length, and the night is about as long as the day. The sun rises at about 6 a.m., and sets at about 6 p.m.

This makes it easy to get into a steady and repeatable routine each day, which makes it easy to get into a steady and repeatable routine, week after week. Along with the pre-dictable weather, this makes it a near-perfect location for steady creative output.

TEN YEARS after my move from San Francisco to Chicago, I had built my perfect weekly routine in Colombia. I was steadily producing my weekly podcast, regularly ship-ping new articles and short books, and making progress on this book. Aside from being in different stages of different projects, every week was a carbon copy of the previous week, and I didn't want to change a thing.

My experiment of moving to build my perfect Creative Cycles had worked so well, after nearly three years in Colombia, I was looking forward to staying. Strolling home one night from the coworking space across the street, excite-ment welled up inside me. I imagined everything I could create in the coming years, even decades. *Who knows how long I can keep this up?* The temperature of the air was perfect, the night was quiet, and, after years of struggle, I was in creative bliss.

But I would soon learn that, while you can create cycles that work with the rhythms of the natural world, your projects, your creative energy, and the cultural cues around you, sometimes, the world simply won't cooperate. My life, and my Creative Cycles, were about to get thrown into a blender – and it was going to put my creative output in serious jeopardy.

CREATIVE SYSTEMS

I must create a system,
or be enslaved by another man's.

—WILLIAM BLAKE

OCTOBER 31, 2018 – Panama City, Panama. My luck keeps getting worse. There's a gigantic spike digging a hole next to my building. It's like a jackhammer had a child with Optimus Prime, and that child is having a temper tantrum next door. The floor is shaking. The plates in the kitchen cabinet behind me are rattling. The only way I can get any work done is to put in ear plugs, then over those ear plugs place noise-cancelling headphones, and through those noise cancelling headphones blast sound from a white noise app.

With this combination, I can accomplish most things I would normally accomplish in my apartment in Medellín. But tomorrow is going to be a problem. Tomorrow, I'm supposed to interview Dr. David Rock for my podcast.

David's book, *Your Brain at Work*, was the first book I read when I began this journey. *Your Brain at Work* gave me a vocabulary with which to understand what was going on in my brain when producing creative work. It helped me understand why I needed to do prioritization and planning separately from the rest of my work. It helped me under-

stand why I got fatigued when I switched mental states. It
helped me understand that I needed to get information into
my long-term memory – off the "stage" and into the
"audience" – before I could connect it with other knowledge
to form breakthrough ideas.

So, six years after reading *Your Brain at Work*, I was excited to finally speak to the author of the book, and share his
knowledge with my listeners. And I couldn't do that with a
howitzer blasting next to me all day.

The pounding started at 7 a.m. this morning. Now 2
p.m., it's still going. It's a safe bet tomorrow at 2 p.m. – when
I'm scheduled to talk to Dr. Rock – this machine will be
repeatedly blasting away at the bedrock next to my building.

What should I do? I asked myself. Since I had arrived only
the night before, I knew nothing about Panama City. I had
barely managed to buy groceries. I was tempted to be upset
at the owner of the apartment, but in all fairness, the Airbnb
listing did warn of construction noise. Looking at the pic-
tures and seeing the giant walk-in closet, I took the gamble
that the walk-in closet would provide enough insulation from
the noise to record a podcast. As it turned out, this walk-in
closet shared a wall with the construction site.

Not that it would have made a difference if the closet was
on the other side of the apartment. This "construction
noise" was much more than "noise." "Noise" is something
you hear. This was seismic activity.

Even if the listing did warn of "noise," I didn't have the
luxury of being picky in selecting a place to stay. After returning to Colombia from a trip to the U.S., I was welcomed

by a surprise: I didn't have as many days left to legally stay in the country as I thought I had. I was staying on a tourist permit, which allowed a certain number of days per year. According to the stamp on my passport, I had eighteen days left. The immigration officer I met with on re-entry into Colombia insisted I had only nine.

Unfortunately, she was right. The immigration officer who stamped my passport on the previous entry had miscounted. You might think that shouldn't matter – that if an officer makes an error, that's their problem, not yours. You might also think that, surely, some technology exists that would prevent such errors. Perhaps something that could add and subtract numbers, thus preventing human error. Something that would "compute." You could call it a "computer." Apparently not.

So, within twenty-four hours of returning to Colombia, I had to get back out of Colombia. I had twenty-four hours to sleep, pack, give an online class I had scheduled, say goodbye to my girlfriend, and – most importantly – find another country where I could hide out for nine days.

That country ended up being Panama. Given the urgency of the situation, I didn't have much time to secure a place to stay. In fact, my booking was so last-minute, I didn't know until I landed in Panama City where I would be sleeping that night.

So, I had rolled the dice on this last-minute apartment. But it turned out I couldn't record an interview from here, and I didn't know where else to go. I let out a deep sigh. I'd have to cancel our interview. I could try to reschedule, I thought, but as difficult as it was to schedule this interview in the first place, that didn't seem likely.

I started typing an email to David's assistant: "Unfortunately, I have to cancel tomorrow's interview." As I typed those words, something changed inside me.

How am I going to explain this? I thought to myself. I didn't want to send the vague "something came up." That would be rude.

And the truth was too complicated. The truth was that six months ago, my Colombian visa had been rejected. It was supposed to be simple: Countries want foreign investors. When a foreign investor meets the requirements, you give them a visa. I had made an investment in a Colombian company. I met the requirements, but my visa application was rejected.

And now I'm stuck in Panama. In eight days, I'll fly back to Colombia and re-apply the next day – the very first day I'm eligible. They'll realize they made a mistake, they'll give me my visa, and this ordeal will be behind me.

But for now, I'm stuck in this broken slot machine that keeps going bust. This is the fifth trip I've taken in the past six months, in order to stay legal. It would have been simpler if there hadn't been a surprise interpretation of the law that cut a month off the days I had left on my tourist permit. It would have been simpler if that immigration officer hadn't written the wrong number of days on my passport. And none of that would have mattered if I hadn't been the recipient of a surprise rejection, due to what, I'll never know. Someone needing to fill a rejection quota? Someone thinking my documents were forged? Someone not liking the way I smiled? The actual reason for my rejection was "privileged information" – which I suspect means, "because we felt like it." Lawyer after lawyer told me, "You won the lottery. I'm sorry."

So for now, I'm on a losing streak. And that losing streak includes – after months of scrambling to find solid soil to stand on – landing on soil that's being pummeled a hundred times a minute by a gigantic steel phallus.

But as I typed my cancellation email, I realized I was letting this losing streak cloud my thinking. *There has to be a solution to this*, I thought. Just because I'm being tossed about by circumstances beyond my control does not mean I have control over nothing. I have control over *this*. I won't let the whims of an immigration agent having a bad day six months ago affect this moment.

I deleted my email draft.

EVEN I was surprised by the positive response to my interview with David Rock. One reviewer of my podcast specifically recommended it, saying, "I particularly loved the David Rock episode. So much knowledge there."

I was surprised, because it was my most difficult interview ever. That had nothing to do with David, and everything to do with my circumstances. I was in a rented conference room in a Panama City coworking space. The office manager gave me the side-glance as I made one request after another. *Do you have more pillows I can pile up on this table, to dampen the echo? Is there anything we can do about this noisy air conditioner? Is it possible to connect via Ethernet, instead of WiFi?*

I had conducted all my remote interviews from the comfort of my home studio in Medellín. Now that I had decided I would do whatever it took to make this interview happen, I wanted to be sure nothing went wrong. Still, with the change in environment and the dark cloud of my visa woes hanging over my head, it took every drop of energy I had to focus on the conversation.

The decision to continue with the interview came in a flash of resilience. But that resilience was only possible because I had the mental energy left over to fuel that resilience. I had that mental energy because I had ways of managing it, even when things didn't go as planned. I had Creative Systems.

Creative Systems are repeatable processes that help you bring creative works from idea through execution. By formalizing parts of the creative process and turning them into actionable steps, Creative Systems save mental energy. Through repetition, Creative Systems help you ship more work, and higher-quality work, in less time, and with less energy.

The mere idea of Creative Systems may seem like a contradiction. As we've explored throughout this book, the creative process is characterized by unpredictability. It's true you can't predict what you'll find in the course of the creative process. But with practice, you can predict how you'll arrive at the final solution.

MORE THAN ONE CUPCAKE

Think of Creative Systems like baking a batch of cupcakes. You pour your batter into the cupcake tin. The cupcake tin has a series of molds for the batter. Some cupcake batter has coloring, or different ingredients, such as poppy seeds or blueberries. Once the cupcakes are baked, you add different types of frosting, or toppings such as colored sprinkles. You even use the same frosting on each cupcake, while applying that frosting in a different design.

Each mold in the cupcake tin is the same size and shape. Each cupcake is baked for the same amount of time and at the same temperature. Yet you now have a huge variety of cupcakes, each characterized by its own unique colors, flavors, and textures.

I was able to focus my attention, and find a way to make my interview with David Rock happen, because I knew exactly what it would mean to miss that interview: Not only would I miss an interview I had been trying to secure since I had started my podcast three years prior, I also knew if I missed this interview, I would miss a week of my podcast.

That wasn't a straightforward calculation to make. I knew I would be in Panama City, with this machine pounding next to me, for eight more days. I knew that, from Panama City, I would fly to Bogotá for my visa interview, then back to Medellín. While I was confident my visa application would finally be accepted, I couldn't be sure. If my visa application was rejected, I would have to scramble once again to find soil to stand on and a roof to put over my head. All this flying around and this uncertainty meant that even if

I were able to reschedule the interview, it wouldn't be possible to have the episode ready for its scheduled release date.

I was able to see what would happen if I missed that interview, and I was able to find the mental energy and resilience to find a solution, because I had a schedule to look at, and reliable to-do items in my task management system.

Before I had Creative Systems, I produced each episode as it came. Time and time again, I thought about how much research to do and what questions to ask. I didn't have a process to follow. I had to switch to and from the Prioritize mental state over and over. I was making one cupcake at a time: putting my single-cupcake tin in the oven, guessing a temperature to bake it at, then checking over and over to see if it was done yet.

If I had been producing my podcast "one-cupcake-at-a-time" during the time I was in Panama City, I would have been leaking an enormous amount of creative energy. With all the other stressors I had going on in my life, I would have given up on the interview, and my three-year streak of delivering a podcast episode each Thursday morning would have been broken.

Fortunately, just as my visa troubles had begun six months prior, I had started to implement Creative Systems into my production process. The chaos of those six months put pressure on me to make those systems bulletproof.

Creative Systems harness the power of Creative Cycles. Creative Cycles are the trips your creative works take through the Four Stages of Creativity. Creative Systems are the itinerary for taking those trips. When will you arrive at each destination, how long will you stay, and what mode of transportation will you take to get to the next destination? These questions are all answered by the Creative System.

MINIMUM CREATIVE DOSE

The essential building block of Creative Systems is what I call the Minimum Creative Dose. The Minimum Creative Dose is inspired by a concept in medicine – the minimum effective dose. The minimum effective dose – as the name implies – is the smallest dose you can take of a medication – the *minimum dose* you can take of that medication – to get an *effect* from that medication. And so, the Minimum Creative Dose is the smallest action you can take on a creative project to make progress on that project.

We've already learned a lot in this book about the power of Incubation. That even when you aren't actively working on a creative project, you are still making progress on a creative project. Your Passive Genius is consolidating memories, forgetting bad ideas, and even working to find good ideas. This all happens whether you're sleeping, working on another project, or merely staring at the wall.

But your Passive Genius has nothing to work with – nothing to incubate – if you don't first give it raw materials. This is where the Minimum Creative Dose comes in.

The power of the Minimum Creative Dose highlights an important way that creative productivity differs from traditional productivity. It has to do with open loops.

When you're simply trying to get things done, open loops are your enemy. The beauty of productivity systems that enhance traditional productivity – such as the system literally called *Getting Things Done* – is that they prevent open loops.

For example, you don't want to think about buying cat food when you aren't at the grocery store. That would be an open loop. Instead, you want to store that idea in a "trusted system," as *Getting Things Done* author, David Allen would call it. You need to trust that when you're at the grocery store, you'll remember to buy cat food. The moment you think of buying cat food, that goes on your shopping list, and you can trust that when you're at the grocery store, you will remember to buy cat food.

As soon as cat food goes on your grocery list, the open loop of thinking about buying cat food is closed. Your mental resources are now free to focus on other things.

Open loops are your enemy when it comes to traditional productivity. Open loops remind you to do things that you can't currently do. But when it comes to creative productivity, open loops are a gift. Open loops give your Passive Genius something to work with. The way to get the most out of Incubation, with minimal conscious effort, is by using the Minimum Creative Dose.

To see the Minimum Creative Dose in action, try this experiment: The next time you have an idea for something – whether it's a short story, a painting, or a song – give your Passive Genius the Minimum Creative Dose. Jot down just a few things, make a sketch, or hum a few bars into a recorder. Set a timer for two minutes if it helps. Then, forget about it. Go about whatever you were doing.

Now, set a reminder. Remind yourself to revisit this idea

CREATIVE SYSTEMS   185

the next day. Work on it again, just for a few minutes. It will be easier to make progress than it was the day before.

When I work on only a small portion of a big project during my weekly review, as we talked about in the previous chapter, I'm using the Minimum Creative Dose. I do that because the Minimum Creative Dose is especially powerful when working on tough creative problems. Tough creative problems are easy to procrastinate on, but not when you commit to the Minimum Creative Dose. You can't justify procrastinating on something that only takes a couple minutes. When you commit to working on a problem for only a couple minutes, it prevents – as I talked about in *The Heart to Start* – "Inflating the Investment." You can't talk yourself out of making progress by making the excuse that you don't have time.

When you're working on your toughest creative problems, that's when you need Incubation the most. There are so many loose ends to consider, you'll create a logjam if you try to power through the problem all at once. The Minimum Creative Dose helps you activate those loose ends. It helps you create open loops. As you go about your day, work on other projects, or even sleep, your subconscious is working with the Minimum Creative Dose you've given it.

Additionally, having open loops on your creative projects opens you up to random source materials that you encounter throughout your day. Consider the story Dr. Robert Maurer told me on my podcast. Dr. Maurer specializes in helping his therapy patients make progress through very tiny steps. In fact, he wrote a book called *One Small Step*.

At one of his seminars, Dr. Maurer asked his students a question: What color was the car two cars over from where you parked this morning? Of course, nobody knew the answer. He asked them again the next day, and a few people knew the answer. By the third day, everyone knew the answer. By asking the question, he had created an open loop. They couldn't help but notice the color of the car two cars over.

It's like the Baader-Meinhof phenomenon: When you learn a new word, suddenly, you start to notice it everywhere. Once the word is planted in your subconscious, you start to notice it in places where you normally would have ignored it. Once a creative problem is planted in your subconscious, you more easily notice the solution when you happen upon it.

(The Baader-Meinhof phenomenon, by the way, is named after the Baader-Meinhof gang – a far-left German revolutionary terrorist group that was active in the 1970s, '80s, and '90s. Never heard of them? Now you'll see them everywhere.)

Think about how Charles Goodyear discovered the process for vulcanizing rubber. He accidentally spilled rubber mixed with sulfur on a hot stove and noticed that the combination of heat and sulfur had changed the quality of the rubber. He was able to recognize the opportunity this presented only because he already had the problem implanted in his mind. He had an open loop. He had spent five years trying to create a rubber that wouldn't get brittle in cold weather and sticky in hot weather.

I used the power of the Minimum Creative Dose when I was first learning Spanish. Conceptual artist and neuroscientist Daniel J. Wilson encouraged me to watch the first twenty minutes of a movie in Spanish each day. I watched the same twenty minutes of the same movie every morning, with breakfast.

The first week, nothing happened. I was hearing more-or-less nonsense speech as I ate my breakfast. Occasionally, I'd look up and read the English subtitles that accompanied the sounds I was hearing.

But eventually, really amazing things did happen. Nonsense sound bites from the movie were stuck in my head, the same way a melody might get stuck in my head. Those nonsense sound bites began to take on meaning. As I went about my day, living in Colombia, I found myself referring to those sound bites. I'd tell myself, *In the movie, they say it* this *way, so maybe I'll say it* that *way.* Eventually, I changed my habit so that instead of English subtitles, the movie displayed Spanish captions. Those nonsense sound bites had taken on enough meaning for me to connect them to written words.

Many people have tried to learn languages by watching movies. But unless you're at an advanced level of the language, you won't make progress. You don't recognize the sound patterns well enough to get value out of watching one movie after another. But when you watch the same segment of the same movie over and over, your Passive Genius gets a chance to recognize those patterns. If you give it the Minimum Creative Dose, the times in between those doses become productive.

CYCLES IN SYSTEMS

By the time I was in Panama City, I had my processes for producing my podcast broken down into Creative Systems. I knew as long as I followed the tasks in my task management system, each episode would progress through the Four Stages of Creativity, and reach completion. Plus, those tasks were reduced to the Minimum Creative Dose, so they were easy to tackle.

Additionally, my Creative Systems were built along with the rhythms of Creative Cycles, so I could get maximum creative output with minimum effort.

I conducted my interviews on a cycle. As I mentioned in the previous chapter, there are times of year when guests are less likely to be available for interviews. In the beginning of the year, people are more focused on their new goals for the year, and being on podcasts is usually not one of those goals. Additionally, in the summer, many people are traveling and/or on vacation.

I realized that if I aimed to do one interview a week, during two different three-month "seasons," I would have enough interviews to last the whole year (with interview episodes going live every other week). So, I try to do an interview a week during March, April, and May; and again I try to do an interview a week during September, October, and November. (December is another month when it's difficult to schedule interviews. Besides, I like to create space during December. I like to take advantage of the cultural cue of the winter holidays, which marks a yearly Creative Cycle, to get deeper into that fragile insightful state John Konious talked about in the previous chapter. This helps me reevaluate my direction and get ready for the New Year.)

So, in the yearly cycle, the Creative System for my podcast looks like this:

INTERVIEW "SEASONS"

Mar   Sep

My Creative System for podcast production works on a monthly cycle as well. The final week of each month, I prepare all episodes for production for the following month. But before those episodes are ready for production, I need to record the intros. I record intros on the previous week – the second-to-last week of the month. The week before that, I write draft scripts for the intros.

So, on the monthly cycle, my Creative System for producing my podcast looks like this:

PODCAST WORK
BY WEEK IN MONTH

Within that monthly cycle are my weekly cycles. I've already mentioned that I try not to work on the podcast on

Mondays. The day I do spend the most time on the podcast is Thursday. I especially try to schedule all interviews on Thursdays.

So, on the weekly cycle, my Creative System for producing the podcast looks like this:

PODCAST WORK
BY DAY IN WEEK

Mon   Fri

Within those weekly cycles are the individual days of the week. Within those days, if I'm going to work on the podcast, I'll do so in the afternoons.

So, if I'm scheduling an interview, I always try to schedule it on a Thursday afternoon. Usually, this works for my guests, but I do sometimes end up doing interviews on Wednesday or Friday afternoons. If there's an extreme mismatch in schedule – for example if my guest is in Europe – I'll sometimes have to do an interview earlier, such as in the late morning.

When I prepare an entire month's episodes in a single afternoon, I'm doing what's called "batching." Instead of making a single cupcake, I'm baking an entire tray. Batching is nothing new. Many people are familiar with the concept of producing a large number of one product at a time. Industry is based upon batching – it's how we're able to produce incredible items such as cars or smartphones, at very low costs.

Batching is easy to do when producing a large number of items that are exactly the same. But when you're producing creative works, batching is much harder. For many years, I understood the idea of batching, but I never had the energy to actually do it. I'd tell myself, *Maybe next time*, while struggling through the process of producing only one blog post, or only one podcast episode.

CREATIVE WORK is different from procedural work because it demands a respect for the Four Stages of Creativity. Creative Systems are different from other processes, because Creative Systems also demand a respect for the Four Stages. So, building Creative Systems demands a different mindset toward batching.

I was once telling a friend about the Creative Systems I used to produce my podcast. I told him I had process documents, with checklists of steps to follow. He said, "oh, you mean SOPs – Standard Operating Procedures."

I bristled at the idea of calling my processes Standard Operating Procedures. They were something different, to me. "Yeah, SOPs" I said, and smiled. "*Sloppy* Operating Procedures."

SOP: SLOPPY OPERATING PROCEDURE

Sloppy Operating Procedures are living documents. You approach them with the mindset that they are always changing – they are never done. So, they're anything but "standard."

If I ever have trouble sleeping, I'll be sure to tell myself that I'm going to write a Standard Operating Procedure. The mere idea of the task is too daunting. I'm supposed to come up with a step-by-step, *standard*, way of producing something that requires creativity? It feels impossible.

Standard Operating Procedures are at odds with creative work, but Sloppy Operating Procedures work in harmony with the creative process. They're actually fun to create, and they save creative energy.

Every time I create something, I open a Sloppy Operating Procedure document. The first couple times I'm creating the thing, my SOP is nothing more than quick notes I jot down. Some notes are mere questions I'm asking myself. Other notes are steps I might be able to repeat in the future. Other notes are an attempt to formalize the building blocks of the creative work. My SOP is full of misspellings and incomplete sentences. My Sloppy Operating Procedure is – well – *sloppy*.

For example, my Sloppy Operating Procedure helps me write intro scripts for my podcast interviews. These intros are the few minutes at the beginning of each episode, where I tell listeners what the conversation will be about, and get them excited to listen to it. I also make some announcements, and include messages from my sponsors.

The *Standard* Operating Procedure approach would be like so: I would copy and paste the bio from the guest's website, then I would read that bio, word-for-word. I might sprinkle in some standard phrases – so overused as to be meaningless – such as "I'm excited to have our guest today," and "let's dive in!"

If I'm a little more motivated, I might say a few things about the interview. Since I'd be following the *Standard* Operating Procedure, to make things easier on myself, I would simply ask the same questions of each guest during each interview. If I wanted to write some teasers into my intro, I could grab some of the guest's answers to those questions.

This would make it easy to write podcast intros and prepare for interviews, and some podcasts actually operate this way. Following a format like this for writing intros is a step up from having no intro at all, but it's boring, and it makes for a boring podcast. It's like making a huge batch of vanilla cupcakes, with vanilla frosting.

But it's not good for my listeners, and, frankly, it's not good for me as a podcast producer, either. I want to learn from my guests, and I want to share what I've learned with my listeners. I need to internalize what the conversation is about, and pull out those lessons. I need to package them so my listeners can learn – in one listen – what it took me hours of preparation and multiple listens to learn myself. Every cupcake is different from the previous cupcake.

The first several times I wrote an intro, my Sloppy Operating Procedure looked like this:

[How can I best write intros for the podcast? I need to have a good understanding of what's discussed in the interview. What are the key insights? What are good sound bites that can be repurposed into social media clips, or used as a teaser at the beginning of the episode?]

The brackets are literally in the SOP. Remember, the SOP is *sloppy*, and brackets give me permission to write incomplete thoughts.

THE POWERFUL POWER OF REPETITION

In the beginning, I tried to write my intro scripts in one sitting. I sat at my computer and listened to the episode, all along trying to think of what to say about it. Eventually, I learned that the process was easier if I gave myself the Minimum Creative Dose, and let my Passive Genius do most of the work for me.

Now, I listen to an interview several times before I write the intro. But there's much less drudgery involved in the process now. I don't have to sit at my computer and listen to the interview. Instead, I load it up on a mobile app, and listen while I do other things. Multitasking generally doesn't work. But while the interview is playing, I'm doing tasks that don't require much conscious effort. In his book, *Indistractable*, Nir Eyal calls this "multichannel multitasking," because it uses different mental resources or "channels." I listen while I cook, eat, shower, or go for a walk. I listen to each interview about three times.

As I did with the movie clip I watched over and over while learning Spanish, I don't force myself to pay attention to the interview. I know that in the course of listening to it a few times, the right insights will come to me. By the third time I listen, I have an intuitive sense of what parts of the conversation are interesting, or what parts need to be cut. Additionally, I can listen to the interview on a faster speed each time, and still understand what's being said. Through the process of Incubation, the sound patterns have seeped into my long-term memory.

Throughout the process of listening to the interview

multiple times, I make progress on writing the intro script. The first time I listen, I intentionally don't take notes, but the second or third time I listen, whenever I come across an important insight, I jot down a quick note.

By the time I sit down to write an intro script, the hardest part of the job is already done – and I did it while doing other things! I have a list of interesting insights from the conversation. Now, I can write a quick rough draft, using those insights as building blocks.

Taking the Minimum Creative Dose makes the process of writing my intro scripts much easier. Additionally, thinking according to the Minimum Creative Dose helps me respect the Four Stages of Creativity, and work according to mental state.

Before I started using Creative Systems, when I tried to simply sit down and write the intro, I wasn't getting much Preparation. Even when I did find insights I wanted to mention in my script, they didn't get enough Incubation for me to easily write them into the script. Also, I was switching mental states too rapidly. I was listening to the episode, in the Explore mental state, and trying to switch back and forth between that and the Generate mental state.

I use the Minimum Creative Dose not only for finding the insights from my podcast conversations, but also for the act of writing the intro scripts themselves. In my task management system, I have several to-do items for each intro script: one for writing the draft, another for revising the draft, a third one for finalizing the script, and a fourth for recording it. These items are strategically spaced out to allow for Incubation.

Because I leave enough room for Incubation, each of these items is a very quick task. In fact, my to-do item for writing the first draft literally says, "Spend 5 minutes drafting intro." Instead of sitting down and listening to the episode while trying to force out a script, I write the script in three five-minute bursts, spaced out to allow for Incubation. I do the listening that provides the building blocks for the scripts as I go about my day. What used to take an hour, while switching from one mental state to another, now only takes fifteen total minutes of focused work.

By repeating this process, writing intro scripts gets easier. This is true of anything you do repeatedly. Consider what podcast pioneer Ira Glass said when he was being interviewed for the *Longform* podcast. Toward the end of the interview, host Max Linsky asked Glass if he wanted to keep going. Glass said, "I gave you a perfect ending," referring to a comment he had just made. Glass then admitted that he'd been editing the conversation in his head as it happened. At Max's request, Ira recalled key points of the conversation, describing where it got slow, where there were irrelevant details, what parts of the conversation needed to be moved, and what parts needed to be cut completely. After years of editing stories for audio, it's so automatic for Glass that he can't turn it off – even if he's not the one who will do the editing.

OUT OF all the things I've learned producing my podcast, the most valuable thing I've learned is how to use Creative

Systems. I hadn't used Creative Systems to write my first book, or any blog posts I wrote, or any design work I did. That's because it's much easier to develop Creative Systems if you're making something over and over, on a schedule.

Because I was producing a new podcast episode every week, I was able to develop and follow Creative Systems. I was able to start with a Sloppy Operating Procedure, and, each week, improve upon that procedure. I was able to break down the process into Minimum Creative Doses, and experiment with how much Incubation I needed to prepare for interviews and write scripts.

It's only through this repetition that I've been able to identify the best way to work with Creative Cycles, and to build Creative Systems, so I can batch my production on a monthly basis.

My Creative Systems for producing the podcast are so refined I now have an automation for generating tasks for each episode. As soon as I enter my air date and record date into my production spreadsheet, an automation generates the tasks in my task management software.

I know that as long as I follow the due dates in my task management system, my Passive Genius will make enough progress between tasks for me to arrive at a solution. I don't have to second-guess my schedule and switch to the Prioritize mental state. When a crisis comes along, I have more mental energy left over to adjust, or to find the mental fortitude to press on.

Creative Systems are easier to develop and implement on smaller creative works that you repeat frequently. But now that I'm well-practiced in using Creative Systems, I'm able to apply the same thinking to much larger projects. Each time I write a book, for example, I open up my Sloppy Operating Procedure and think about how to formalize the process. I haven't repeated the process enough times to have a strict system, but it does prevent drudgery. For example, I don't have to figure out – once again – how to best format a book for publication.

Once I've formalized the Creative System for producing a particular type of creative work, I'm able to produce more of the creative work – at a higher level of quality – with less energy. I then have more energy left over to produce other creative works. Through Creative Systems, I've transferred the process from the "front burner" to the "back burner."

FRONT BURNER/BACK BURNER

You often hear people talk about putting a project on the "back burner." What they mean is they have abandoned the project until further notice. They aren't making progress on it – other than Incubation that might happen while they're taking a break – if they return to the project at all.

But if you're cooking something, and you put it on the back burner, you haven't abandoned it. You've simply reached a state at which you can keep cooking it, with little active intervention. If you're boiling pasta, for example, you can put it on the back burner. You know to stir it once in a while, and you know you can start checking on it in about seven minutes, to get it *al dente*.

The first several times you produce a creative work, you

need to keep it on the front burner. It requires your best creative energy. It's like you're stir-frying vegetables, and you want to get them just right. But once you get your Creative Systems set up, you can put that project on the back burner. It doesn't require your best creative energy. You're still cooking, but you know exactly how much – or little – of your active attention it requires.

When I started my podcast, it was very much a front-burner project. It took my best creative energy to produce each episode. I didn't have much skill or experience in preparing for interviews or writing intro scripts. I didn't know where to put the theme music, or what theme music would give the show the right mood. I hadn't determined the best process for publishing the episode to the various podcast directories, or how best to format the blog posts. I had to make all these decisions for every episode, and I made them in real-time.

Now that I have Creative Systems for my podcast, it's a back-burner project. I know if I follow the tasks in my task management system, I'll produce the episode on time, at a high level of quality. I have checklists for setting up my recording equipment, I have checklists for my production team to follow to publish the episodes, I have a spreadsheet to give my team everything they need to take the show live, I have a spreadsheet for generating and scheduling social media updates, and I have an email automation for notifying my email subscribers.

This has a profound effect on what I can do with my front-burner creative energy. When my podcast was a front-burner project, the morning my podcast went live, my front-burner energy was consumed by the podcast. I was busy publishing the episode, promoting it on social media, and making sure it was showing up in all the podcast directories.

Now that my podcast is a back-burner project, my front-burner energy is available to work on other projects. On the days when my podcast goes live, I don't think about it at all. It's often not until the afternoon that I say to myself, *Oh yeah! That episode went live today, didn't it?* Instead of scrambling to take an episode live, I've spent my entire morning – my Creative Sweet Spot – on a front-burner project.

REPEATING STEPS to produce different versions of similar creative works also saves creative energy, because the sequence of actions get stored in your memory. In *Your Brain at Work*, David Rock explains that "your basal ganglia recognize, store, and repeat patterns in your environment." A routine that you follow to produce something is essentially a pattern. When I tell myself, *listen to the interview while in the Explore mental state and take a note when you hear something interesting*, over time, the guidelines I've put on my thinking become easier to replicate. When you repeat a routine your brain begins the process of "long-term potentiation" in as few as three iterations. Rock calls this process "hardwiring."

Your brain is so good at recognizing these patterns, it can happen without your conscious awareness. Study participants who were instructed to press buttons in a patterned sequence responded ten percent faster than those who had to respond to random sequences. What's more surprising is the pattern was so complex the participants had no idea the pattern was there. They couldn't consciously recall a sequence had repeated during the experiment, yet they still pressed the buttons faster. As Rock explained, "their basal ganglia had noticed the patterns implicitly, but the volunteers could not explicitly identify them."

When you're using Creative Systems, you aren't making identical cupcakes, but you also aren't constructing elaborate, sculptural, multi-tiered wedding cakes. To build Creative Systems, you need to resist the urge to make every creative work perfectly customized. You need to make creative constraints.

CREATIVE CONSTRAINTS

Most people don't like the sound of constraints. It sounds like you're not getting what you want. But you are getting what you want. Good constraints trade something you only *kind of* want for something you *really* want.

When you build Creative Systems, you need to standardize parts of your creative process. Those parts of the process never change. That constraint can feel stifling if you let it. But if you embrace that constraint, it actually frees up your energy to focus on the work.

When cars were first being made, each car was made by hand. One car might look like the next car, but they were actually quite different. Because the parts were made by hand, you couldn't switch one part out from one car with the same part from another car. There were tiny differences in the dimensions of the parts. These differences didn't add up to much when comparing parts, but when comparing cars, they made a big difference. One car of the same model would be bigger or smaller than another car of the same model. If one part was smaller on one car, then the rest of the parts needed to be smaller, too – so the entire car was smaller.

Now, parts on cars are interchangeable. The production process is standardized, so the people designing the cars aren't touching the final product. They have to make the production process part of their design considerations. Each individual car may lack that hand-made touch, but the cars are more affordable.

IN MOVING my podcast production from the front burner to the back burner, I had to make lots of compromises. At first, I wanted to arrange every episode by feel – maybe the intro music would start in one place in one episode, and at another place in another episode. But to make production efficient, I eventually had to standardize the placement of the intro music.

The hardest thing to let go of was being able to record intros as episodes were published. If I had a personal update or something to promote in my business, when I was recording a fresh intro each week I could simply slip my announcement into that week's intro. Now that I batch episodes on a monthly basis, I can't do that. When I'm recording an intro, it might be a whole month before it's actually published.

Making that compromise has costs, but the trade-off is worth it. I get more work done with less energy. One could argue it reduces quality, but in some ways it has improved quality. It forces me to be more organized. Instead of flying by the seat of my pants, I now have designated slots within the intros in certain weeks of the month for making certain announcements. Some weeks, I thank the supporters of the show, other weeks, I thank listeners who share the show on social media, still other weeks, I showcase what listeners are creating.

The compromises you make depend upon the goal of what you're creating. If I were creating an industry news podcast, it wouldn't make sense for me to batch production on a monthly basis. I'd make compromises in other ways, such as by standardizing my process for deciding what news to cover. I might even choose those standards so the news I'd cover wouldn't be outdated on a weekly production cycle.

Standardization can obviously go too far. Surely you've tried to make something out of LEGO bricks, only to find you couldn't achieve your vision. There are only so many different blocks, so you can only do so many things. The key to standardization is to create constraints that will make your production process smoother, without compromising the essence of what you're trying to achieve. If you choose your constraints wisely, they can actually enhance creativity. Robert Frost said writing in free verse is like playing tennis with the net down. He had better ideas because he was following poetry's constraints.

Since you're using a Sloppy Operating Procedure to standardize your process, you don't have to decide all at once what compromises to make. As long as you're making similar creative works over and over, you get new opportunities to decide which trade-offs work best for your goals.

Once I set up the systems for producing my podcast well enough that I could produce it with back-burner energy, I used my leftover front-burner energy to create a weekly email newsletter. Like many authors with email lists, I struggled to keep consistent content going out to my subscribers. In producing my podcast, I had learned how Creative Systems helped me produce content consistently, so I applied everything I had learned to producing a consistent newsletter.

But I didn't want to let my vision of a perfectly-repeatable newsletter system get in the way of progress. I had a lot of things to decide, and I didn't want to get creatively blocked trying to make everything perfect.

FLY HIGH WITH PILOTS

So, my *Love Mondays* newsletter started off with "pilots." You've heard of pilots being used in television production. In television, a pilot is a test episode of a show, created to decide whether or not to produce more episodes. You can use pilots the same way to begin producing Creative Systems.

None of my newsletter subscribers knew the first editions of *Love Mondays* were pilots. In fact, those first editions weren't called *Love Mondays*. To start building a Creative System, I knew there were variables I needed to experiment with: I needed to pick a day of the week, I needed a reliable source of content, and I needed a repeatable format I could use for developing that content.

I chose the day of the week by process of elimination. My podcast episodes were already coming out on Thursdays, and I wanted to reserve the middle of the week – Tuesdays and Wednesdays – for sending emails during product launches, since those are the days with the highest engagement, as we talked about in the previous chapter. There were already a couple of well-known newsletters in my space that were associated with certain days of the week: for example, Tim Ferriss has *Five-Bullet Fridays*, and Paul Jarvis has *The Sunday Dispatches*.

Internally, I called the first several pilots of my weekly newsletter *Friday Night Highlights*. From years of reading hundreds of books, I have more than 15,000 highlights electronically stored. For the first several editions of my weekly newsletter, I experimented with sharing one interesting highlight, along with my thoughts on the highlight. As implied by my internal pilot name of *Friday Night Highlights*, I sent these first editions on Friday evenings. Again, none of my email subscribers knew what was going on. They had signed up to get emails, but up to this point, I still didn't have a consistent schedule.

As I produced these pilot emails, I was keeping a Sloppy Operating Procedure document, and filling it with my thoughts. I was asking myself questions, such as *Can I come up with an interesting highlight each week?*, *Do I want to share only highlights?*, and *How can I break apart the components of each newsletter so they fit in a spreadsheet?*

By asking these questions, I ended up deciding that a name that included "highlights" was too restrictive. For example, sometimes I wanted to share my own thoughts, rather than something I had read in a book. Thanks to the flexibility of producing pilots, I was able to change the format of my newsletter.

Now, the production of my newsletter is on a "back-burner" Creative System. On a monthly basis, I collect together highlights or other thoughts I want to share, and fill out a spreadsheet with all the relevant information. My team uses the information in that spreadsheet, along with process and formatting standards, to produce and schedule the newsletter.

When I do have front-burner energy left over, I use it to tweak my newsletter. I document changes in my Sloppy Operating Procedure to update the Creative System and keep improving the newsletter. My newsletter will probably be different by the time you read this. Sign up at kdv.co/newsletter to find out.

Like my podcast production process, my newsletter production process has repeatable tasks, broken up according to the Minimum Creative Dose. I know if I do those easy tasks, I'll produce an entire month's newsletters with a small amount of focused work.

A COUPLE weeks after I had found the fortitude to keep my interview appointment with David Rock, I was asking myself, *How the hell did I end up here?!* I was changing my clothes in the filthy bathroom of a laundromat in Chicago.

WHY AM I CHANGING MY CLOTHES
IN A FILTHY LAUNDROMAT BATHROOM?

The immediate answer to how I ended up there was simple: After nine days in Panama City, two days in Bogotá, and a long weekend spent awaiting a decision on my visa application, my lawyer called me. "Your application has been rejected," he said with a sigh. Again, neither of us had any way of knowing why.

I said goodbye to my girlfriend once again, for the fourth emergency trip of the year. I needed to spend the remaining seven weeks of the year outside of Colombia, and I needed to leave tomorrow.

I flew to Chicago, and – at the apartment I reserved there – I would have rather had a jackhammer pounding in the middle of the living room. Instead, after sitting on the couch in that living room, I discovered that couch was visibly crawling with bedbugs.

I spent the next twenty-four hours disinfecting everything I had with me – the majority of my worldly possessions. This meant I had to put all my clothes in an industrial-strength dryer – the kind of high-heat dryer you only find in laundromats that have filthy bathrooms. And since I couldn't risk tracking one bug or one egg anywhere, when I was done with one load, I had to do a second load – to disinfect the clothes I was wearing.

So that was the immediate answer to the question, *How the hell did I end up here?!* But when I was done standing on my own shoes as I changed my pants, so as not to get my socks wet with the unidentified liquid on the floor, I had to look in the scratched and graffitied mirror of that bathroom and ask myself for the deeper answer to the question, *How the hell did I end up here?!* What chain of decisions put me in this situation where it felt as if God or the Universe or Randomness was trying to kill me? And what values guided those decisions?

I came to the conclusion this was all worth it. That as terrible as this situation was, I wouldn't change a single decision – except of course choosing a different apartment in Chicago. After all, I was possessed with the need to create. I had too many unrealized ideas within me, and this life I was building was the only way I could consistently make those ideas a reality. The life where I couldn't do that was a life wherein I wouldn't want to live at all.

I STILL remember the day I got back into the rhythm I had created – where I was consistently in an uninterrupted weekly routine. Where I was masterfully transitioning from one mental state to another, pushing work forward within Creative Cycles, making the most of my energy with well-constructed Creative Systems.

As I went to bed that night, I reflected on everything I had gone through to get to this point of creative bliss: The agony of suffering through writing my first book, the research I had done to better understand the creative process, and two years of building a life and getting settled in Colombia, followed by a year of visa purgatory.

When I was changing my clothes in the filthy bathroom of that laundromat in Chicago, I thought I had hit rock-bottom. But rock-bottom turned out to be at yet another depth. At the age of thirty-nine, I spent the remaining six weeks of the year living with my parents in Phoenix – in a retirement community.

But now, as I sat on the edge of my bed, that was behind me – just an "all is lost" moment in my journey. The moment when the villain had me right where he wanted me, dangling from the edge of a skyscraper.

Yet I had survived. Thanks to the mind management techniques I had developed, and the Creative Systems I had built, I still created consistently. Throughout all of this, I didn't miss an episode of my weekly podcast.

And now, I had just been granted a three-year visa to stay in Colombia. I could finally stop worrying about being able to stay in the place I called home. With this life I had built, my mind danced with visions of what I could achieve in the next three years, and the next thirty years. I had mastered my creativity, and I was living a consistent life, with consistent creative output.

Believe it or not, as I went to bed that night – July 3, 2019 – I said out loud to myself, "I love this life." I said it twice: "I love this life." Tense bands of muscle melted in my jaw, my face, and my neck, as I sunk into bed. I slept better than I had slept in more than a year.

I say, "believe it or not," because the timing was so tragic, it sounds made up. Things were about to get worse than they had ever been. And it was going to start the very next day.

CHAPTER 7

CREATING IN CHAOS

*Invention, it must be humbly admitted,
does not consist in creating out of void but
out of chaos.*

—MARY SHELLEY

JULY 4, 2019 – It's another beautiful day in Medellín. I wake up, do my one-hundred-word routine on my AlphaSmart, meditate, and begin to write. Four hours later, I'm immersed in the words, but ready to pull myself back into the world.

Long, focused writing sessions are like floating in a sensory deprivation tank. You hear nothing, you see nothing, you feel nothing. Your entire experience consists of your own thoughts, which are being effortlessly recorded on the page. It's the first time I've felt this way since my visa troubles started more than a year prior.

I'm finally ready to take this book you're reading into the home stretch – a "theory of everything" for the flawless management of creative energy. My own personal handbook for living an uninterrupted creative life – for reducing the rough grit of life's pesky details down to smooth, silky, frictionless surfaces. Mere slides that send you slipping to your creative destiny.

These first moments after a good session aren't unlike the first moments of consciousness in the morning. I feel the cool tiles on my bare feet, I feel the breeze brush the hairs on my forearms, I hear rumbling engines and faint horns and tinny loudspeakers of vendors on the street outside, and I am awake.

I can already taste lunch. My mouth waters as I stroll to my kitchen to cook my first meal of the day.

Today, I often think back to this next moment. It was the moment right after I picked my phone up off the kitchen counter. It was the moment right before I looked at my phone's screen.

That moment was my last moment of blissful ignorance.

THE NEXT thing I knew, I was rushing up winding roads through the Andean foothills. I explained to the taxi driver as politely as I could that, yes, his driving was great – normally it wouldn't be a problem – but could he please speed up? He zig-zagged past busses and trucks and slow cars. He passed a tractor on a two-lane road, with a blind curve ahead. After he narrowly missed a head-on collision with an oncoming vehicle, he quietly celebrated to himself with a fist pump. I got to the airport with barely enough time to buy a ticket at the counter for the last flight that would get me to my destination that day.

By the time I got to Phoenix, she was in the ICU. I approached her bedside slowly, finally taking in the scene I had pictured during my twelve-hour journey. Tubes were snaking out of her throat and arms. A respirator heaved rhythmically while numbers flashed on a screen. One final thin tube, connected to a bag of translucent red liquid, was protruding from the top of her head.

My mother had suffered a spontaneous brain hemor-rhage. She had gone into a deep coma almost immediately. The neurosurgeon told us that in the best-case scenario – if she ever wakes up – she might be walking with a cane in two years.

PHOENIX IS hot. Car batteries last only two years, in-stead of the usual three to five. The LCD screens on gas pumps have flaps over them, to protect them from the sun. Sometimes it's so hot that planes can't take off. They have to unload people and bags to make weight.

The Pope is Catholic, Phoenix is hot, and the height of that heat is in July. So, I find myself in a pickle with my sacred morning routine. Not only am I so worried that it's hard to think of anything other than my mother's condition, but there's suddenly something I should be doing in the morning that is more important than writing, meditating, or anything else.

I know, from having spent the final six weeks of the pre-vious year at my parents' house, that my parents are dedi-cated to their own daily routine: going on a walk. But the timing of that walk depends upon the weather. If it's a cold day, the walk happens in the afternoon. If it's a hot day, the walk happens as early in the morning as possible. In Phoenix, in July, they're all hot days.

So, that first morning in Phoenix, I lay in bed, stared at the ceiling, and agonized over this conflict. On one hand, I recognized that when your mother is on the edge of death, you have every excuse in the world to miss your morning writing routine. On the other hand, excuses are a slippery slope. One day it's *My mother is in a coma.* The next day it's *I didn't sleep well, I woke up hungry,* or *I had to respond to a text message on my phone first thing in the morning.*

Yet, when you know you're going to be sitting at your comatose mother's bedside all day – when you know you're going to be struggling to do anything but cry for the foreseeable future – you need all the exercise and fresh air you can get. And when your seventy-one year old father is down the hall – understandably even more shattered than you are – going on that morning walk, before the sun peeks over Mc-Dowell Mountain and instantly brings the heat index over one-hundred degrees, becomes more than simply important. One could argue it becomes a matter of life and death.

So, as daylight began to creep through my bedroom window, I did something I hadn't done in years. I didn't do my one-hundred-word writing habit on my AlphaSmart. I didn't meditate, and I didn't then immediately start working on my most important creative project – this book.

Instead, I stepped out of bed, put on my workout clothes, slipped on my shoes, and walked out to the living room. My father was sitting in his usual chair, with his coffee mug in hand, and the weight of the world on his brow.

I invited him to go for a walk.

THAT NIGHT, after my father went to bed and I was alone in the stillness of the house, I realized something. It should have been obvious during my year in visa purgatory, but now there was no denying it.

Here I was in my parents' dream house – how different it felt from when I visited it for the first time only three weeks prior. They had moved in three months ago. There were still unpacked boxes, awkward empty spaces that they hadn't yet decided how to furnish, and picture frames leaning against the walls. I slid the palm of my hand over the pink granite kitchen countertop as I approached the documents strewn about its surface.

Peering from the pockets of an open folder were color renderings of the backyard renovation they were planning. I replayed in my mind the saddest image I had seen all day: a delicate yellow string in the backyard, almost blowing away in the wind, but for the pins that stretched it out over the desert gravel. That marked where the pool was to be dug.

But now that renovation was cancelled. Next to the renovation plans lay a brochure for an Alaskan cruise. Next to that, travel insurance claim forms, to cancel the cruise they had planned for the following month.

Everything was in limbo. We were each holding our breath, waiting for what would happen next. Would Mom wake up? Would we have to team up for a long road to recovery? Or would Mom suddenly be gone forever? At this moment, there was no way to know.

What I realized was this: Things don't go as planned. My parents could plan to enjoy their retirement. I could try to design my life around the effortless creative productivity I so badly wanted, but in the end, plans are only plans.

Author Nassim Nicholas Taleb talks about systems that

benefit from chaos. That when something is too rigid, it becomes fragile. If you slam a ceramic coffee mug onto a granite countertop, the mug will shatter. When something benefits from chaos, it's not only flexible enough to withstand stressors – those stressors trigger growth. When you lift weights, you make tiny tears in your muscles, and when those tears heal, your muscles are stronger. Your muscles, unlike the coffee cup, benefit from chaos.

I had been too rigid in building my system for managing creative energy. I had tried to control every tiny aspect of my life. Sometimes it worked, but I was learning the hard way that the Universe didn't always cooperate with my "system."

If my mother didn't die now, she would die at some point in the future. So would my father. So, eventually, would I. And mixed amongst those catastrophic, unpredictable inevitabilities would be countless other minor and unforesee-able inconveniences. Computers would crash, baristas would steep my tea for too long, and visa applications would be rejected.

I was terrified of what would happen if I couldn't keep my morning routine, but ultimately, I needed to be flexible. I hoped to live a creative life, and inherent in that concept is the word *life*. As the Allen Saunders quote goes, "Life is what happens while you're busy making other plans." In other words, things don't go as planned. That is the plan.

If I wanted to live a creative life, I couldn't be so rigid as to become fragile. My system had to be, as the title of one of Taleb's books describes, *Antifragile*.

I would need to be able to create, even when there's

chaos. Better yet, I needed to allow that chaos to become a part of the process. Because – as was now clear – there will always be chaos.

HOW TO KEEP GOING WHEN YOUR LIFE IS A DUMPSTER FIRE

In the days that followed, I set out to muster what creative energy I could. Much of my energy was sapped by grief and worry. The open loop of what would happen to my mother, and how we as a family would cope, was running nonstop.

In this case, there wasn't much I could do about that open loop. Grief inhibits attention and cognitive function. Yes, I had plenty of time, sitting by my mother's bedside, but I barely had the energy to keep myself bathed and fed and active. Not to mention making sure that my father was also keeping himself bathed and fed and active.

The best thing I could do was simply accept that I would get a lot less done than I normally would. I had to ruthlessly prioritize how I would use what little creative energy remained.

I started by clearing away anything that required my front-burner energy. For the foreseeable future, anything that was a one-off project, was my first crack at something new, or required me to talk to people at a given time simply wouldn't get done. I put a potential coaching client on hold, I cancelled meetings, and I was more forgiving of myself for straight up ignoring emails that asked anything of me.

That left my back-burner projects, specifically, my podcast, for which I had consistently delivered a new episode each week for more than three years. On one hand, who cares about your podcast when your mother is dying? Do I merely stop producing episodes, or do I make an announcement to my listeners that I need to take a break? What would I tell them? *Hi, my mom is in a coma and might die, so no more episodes for a while. Bye.* On the other hand, when one major part of your world is falling apart, how can you let the rest of it fall apart, too? I took it as a challenge from the Universe: *The Universe thought it could break my streak by throwing visa troubles and bedbugs at me. It was wrong. And now this bullshit? No way I'm quitting.* I would keep producing episodes.

AT FIRST, the scene surrounding my comatose mother was almost a festive atmosphere. We played her favorite music, watched movies, and rubbed lotion on her hands and feet. It became a spontaneous family reunion. But the nurses' faces told a different story. They half-smiled through looks of concern, as if saying to themselves, "Here we go again. The party phase, before reality sets in."

Each day that went by without my mother's condition improving, her prognosis got worse. After I had asked the doctors the same questions several times, and read all the research papers I could on brain hemorrhages, there was little left to do but wait. I decided to see if I could write some intros for my podcast.

I placed my laptop on the rolling table on which meals were supposed to be served to patients, and opened my task management system. There was a long list of "overdue" tasks, most of which I merely rescheduled for some arbitrary date in the future, when I might be able to think more clearly.

Finally, I was down to my tasks for writing podcast intros. "Draft intro for 5 minutes," one task said. I couldn't think of what to write, but I opened up a document, and started typing in pointless stream of consciousness.

It was hard to accept how bad this writing was, but I thought back to what I had learned from screenwriter Jon Bokenkamp. Jon is the creator of NBC's *The Blacklist*, a thrilling crime series starring James Spader.

I told you in Chapter 3 that Jon writes in stream of consciousness. He explained to me that he'd literally type, *Alright, what's the scene about? We've got a guy.... There's a guy, he's looking through the window at this woman, and we're wondering...* By writing everything, including his own thoughts, he gives himself enough leeway to keep moving.

Before I knew it, I had written not just one draft of an intro script – I had written drafts for all of August. I could feel my spirits lift oh so slightly. I knew if I returned to these scripts in a few days, Incubation would have occurred, and I should be able to make these scripts good enough to record. It was beginning to look like I could keep releasing podcast episodes.

The thing that allowed me to make progress on my projects, even when I had almost no energy to spare, was a special approach I had developed to organizing my tasks.

Yes, I had my tasks broken down by the Minimum Creative Dose. They were spaced out so my Passive Genius could take care of much of the work. But my tasks were also organized so that whatever mental state I was in, I could find tasks I could do in that mental state.

ORGANIZE BY MENTAL STATE

Most of us organize our tasks by project. It's a good way to get a sense of confidence the project is under control. While you're in the Prioritize mental state, simply look over the tasks, confirm the due dates are realistic, and you're ready to get to work.

But when you're using Creative Systems, there's no point to viewing your tasks by project. You already know as long as you hit your due dates, you'll finish the project on time. It doesn't matter what project a task belongs to. What matters is that you can *do* the task. And your ability to do the task depends entirely on your context, in a given moment.

The idea of "context" is a key concept of the *Getting Things Done* system, but it usually refers to your physical context. There are some tasks you can do at home, there are some tasks you can do at the office, and there are some tasks you can do at the grocery store. When you need to buy cat food, you close that open loop by putting it on your grocery list. What makes that grocery list useful is that everything on that list is actionable in the moment you consult that list. You're in the right context: You're in the grocery store.

When you're managing creative energy, contexts aren't only physical – contexts are also mental. If you have fresh creative energy, you're best off doing creative work. If your creative energy is tapped out, you can do some administrative work – or you might be better off taking a break to replenish your energy.

In the time management world, mental context doesn't exist. You're trying to get as many things done in as little time as possible. But in the mind management world, mental context is everything. You may be in the right physical context to write – you're sitting at your desk. You may be in the right temporal context, too – it's working hours, during the week. But it's a waste to try to force yourself to do work you aren't in the right mental state to do.

While sitting at my mother's bedside, it didn't help to have my tasks organized by project. My mental energy was drained, so I couldn't bang away at any task that was put in front of me. Fortunately, I didn't merely have my tasks organized by project – I also had my tasks organized by mental state.

MANY TASK management systems have a "tags" or "labels" feature. (I'll simply call it "tags.") In addition to assigning tasks to a project, you can also attach various tags to each task. You can then view, all at once, all tasks associated with a given tag.

Tags are useful for organizing tasks according to physical context. For example, when I record intros for my podcast, I view all tasks tagged "Recording." I can only record while in my studio – or in front of my portable setup – so it doesn't do me any good to view those tasks in any other context.

Tags are also useful for organizing tasks by mental context. Whenever I create a task, I think about which of the Seven Mental States I'll need to be in to perform that task: Prioritize, Explore, Research, Generate, Polish, Administrate, or Recharge? If it's a project planning task, I attach a "Prioritize" tag. If I need to look something up, I attach a

"Research" tag. Even the automations that generate the tasks in my Creative Systems tag each task with a mental state.

This way, whatever mental state I'm in, I can easily find tasks that match that state. I don't have to switch to the Prioritize mental state – to decide what to do next – then switch again to another mental state, in order to do the task.

While at my mother's bedside, I had no hope of doing anything that required much mental effort. Prioritize and Generate tasks, for example, were out of the question.

However, I could do Explore tasks. Remember, while exploration can involve collecting information associated with a creative problem, the "Explore" mental state is also useful for draft writing. When I'm writing a draft, I'm collecting together all the thoughts I have on a topic. Those thoughts serve as Preparation. Incubation occurs between sessions.

ONCE I had the confidence I could keep my podcast on track, my thoughts returned to this book. When you spend nearly a decade on a project, it messes with your head. It becomes hard to tell the difference between making the product better, and pure procrastination.

One morning, after walking with my father, I decided it was time to return to this book. I had shifted my one-hundred word AlphaSmart habit and my meditation habit to after our morning walk.

Now that those were out of the way, and my dad was in the kitchen eating breakfast, I decided I had some time to work on this book.

DO WHAT YOU CAN WITH WHAT YOU HAVE

Soon, we'd go back to the hospital to meet my brother and his wife for the rest of our new family routine: park the car, sulk across the black asphalt parking lot in 110° heat, maze through the hallways to the ICU – the lyrics of Death Cab for Cutie's "What Sarah Said" playing in my head – and wait next to Mom. I'd sit in my designated spot, where I'd hold her hand, and we'd collectively comment on every twitch of a foot, every choke on the respirator tubes. We'd ask more questions of every nurse who came in the room, as they would explain to us once again that it was just reflexes, that she was still a four on the Glasgow coma scale, and that we still had to wait a few more days to see if her comatose state was due simply to a shock to the brain stem, or irreparable damage.

A part of me wondered if it was right to think about my book at a time like this. Another part reminded myself that times like this are exactly the reason to think about whatever you'd like to contribute to the world during your life. We never know when catastrophe will turn our world upside down, or even end our world.

As I sat at my computer, I reasoned that the fifteen minutes I had wasn't enough. But I reminded myself of my own advice, which I wrote in *The Heart to Start*, that any small amount of time is enough to make a little progress – to not "Inflate the Investment."

Before this emergency trip, I had been consistently writing 1,000, 1,500, even 2,000 words in my morning sessions. I knew I couldn't hold myself to such a standard this morning. *Just do* something *today*, I told myself. *Then do that again tomorrow and the next day. Eventually you'll get somewhere.*

I decided I'd try to write 250 words for this book. It didn't matter if they were good. It didn't matter if I had to completely rewrite them at some future date. All that mattered was I did *something*. Because this was what I had decided to do with my life, because life didn't have guarantees, and because it gave me a sense of meaning. When everything you're experiencing is senseless, you need all the meaning you can get.

Fifteen minutes later, I was surprised by what I had accomplished: The 250 words I wrote came easily. They were more crisp than the words I wrote when I cranked out 1,000 or 2,000 words. They needed very little editing.

Wouldn't that be something, I thought to myself, *if I could actually sit down each morning, write 250 crisp words, and get on with the rest of my day?!* When I wrote my first book, this was exactly what I had *thought* I would be able to do. But I had come to believe that this was an impossible fantasy. I needed to first do the Preparation before I could achieve Illumination.

I HAD been terrified to diverge from my daily routine, but it turned out – to my own surprise – that I was ready to do so. For six years, I had collected the building blocks of a system for managing creative energy; for two more years, I had redesigned my life to perfect that system; and for a year after that, that system had been battle-tested – and battle-improved – by my visa woes. My system had become antifragile. Preparation and Incubation were built into my daily life. Now, I could achieve Illumination easily.

Now, that system was being put to the ultimate test. My mental energy was sapped by grief, and I needed to use what little energy I had as efficiently as possible. In part, that was to keep my business from falling apart, but I remembered that it was also important to be present in the tragedy I was experiencing.

I reminded myself that, as I talked about in *The Heart to Start*, our experiences build up potential energy, which we transform into kinetic energy in the act of creating things. As Ray Bradbury said, "We are cups, constantly and quietly being filled. The trick is, knowing how to tip ourselves over and let the beautiful stuff out."

CREATIVE OPPORTUNITIES

When Jerry Seinfeld and Larry David were producing *Seinfeld*, they insisted their writers' ideas for episodes come from real-life events. They recognized that inherent in life is the chaos that presents us with one creative opportunity after another. By sourcing their situations from real life, they made a show anyone could relate to.

Art is the expression of the chaos of life. In rare cases, chaos presents serendipity. The perfect accident happens at the perfect time. More often, the moment that chaos occurs is anything but the moment in which you can use the opportunities chaos presents.

As Seth Godin has pointed out, many tall buildings in New York City still have water towers on top. Why? Because it's inefficient to pump water upward every time someone opens a faucet. It's more efficient to pump the water up into a water tower, and store it there. Then you can release it on demand, allowing gravity to do the work.

This water-tower-like capture and release of creative opportunities is the job of inboxes in your system. Inboxes store the opportunities that chaos presents, and inboxes save those opportunities until you can use them.

No matter what idea comes to mind, when you have inboxes, you always have a place to put it. When a great idea comes to you while riding the subway, or at lunch with a friend, it can be paralyzing and anxiety-producing. How can you be sure you won't lose this idea?

Since you respect the Four Stages, you know you can't stop what you're doing and see your new idea to completion. Instead, you need to capture the idea, and be confident it won't slip away forever.

The power of inboxes was more apparent than ever as I

responded to my mother's health crisis. In fact, it started on
the plane ride to Phoenix. In the midst of responding to this
tragedy, I struggled to keep a clear head. I knew I was in the
throes of what would become one of the most formative
experiences of my life, but what it meant was still unclear.

Since art is an expression of life, I knew this event would
inform my art in some way – if not for the sake of better art,
at least to help me cope. But it wouldn't be realistic to expect
to remember all the details at some later date, and it would
be even more unrealistic to expect to instantly create mean-
ingful art as it was happening.

While on that plane, which couldn't possibly go fast
enough, there were only so many things I could do. I
couldn't focus on work. I understandably wasn't in the mood
to watch a movie. Just what waited for me at the other end
of my journey was still too abstract to cause me to cry.

So, I pulled out my laptop, and began to write. I sloppily
recorded, beat by beat, everything that had happened thus
far. I captured my thoughts and feelings about potential outcomes. If she died, what would we do? If she needed years
of physical therapy, what would we do?

I didn't do any of this writing in an existing project. I
wrote it in an inbox.

I KEEP numerous inboxes in my system. The "@thisweek"
note I use for my weekly review is one inbox – if I think of
something I need to do during my weekly review, I write a
quick note in that inbox, if it's readily available.

I also have inboxes for each of my projects. Anything I

think about throughout the day for one of my projects, including new ideas, goes in that project's inbox. My Sloppy Operating Procedure documents are all inboxes – if I have an idea for how to improve a process, I put it at the top of the document.

There are two big things that make inboxes powerful: One, inboxes let you close the conscious open loop about an idea. You aren't able to address the idea in the moment, so it goes in an inbox. Two, inboxes give you something to work with when you finally are available to process ideas.

I have inboxes for just about everything. I have a "comedy" inbox, full of things I said off-hand that made people laugh. I have a "Spanish/English interestingness" inbox, full of interesting things I've noticed while learning Spanish. I have a "gifts" inbox. When a loved one tells me about a problem they have, or casually mentions a thing they might like, it goes in the inbox. I don't have to think of gifts when holidays and birthdays come along – I already have a bunch of ideas. I even have a "karaoke songs" inbox. When I sing karaoke, I don't have to rack my brain for ideas of what to sing. I already have a huge list of songs – some songs even have notes next to them about whether or not they've been crowd-pleasers.

So, as I waited for my plane to carry me to Phoenix, I started a new inbox, all for capturing the details of this experience.

WITH ALL these inboxes, you might wonder how I keep track of everything. I have a few different ways of making sure I don't waste mental energy worrying about what's in all my inboxes. The first technique, I call the Creative Cascade.

THE CREATIVE CASCADE

Let's return to the metaphor of ideas as water, only now let's transport ourselves from a concrete jungle full of water towers into an actual jungle, where we see a babbling brook, with a gentle, cascading waterfall. If water is falling down a cascade, it's collecting in a series of pools. My inboxes work like a cascade.

The top of my cascade – the babbling brook – is a tiny pocket notebook I carry around. Whenever I come up with an idea – whether it's a story I want to use in a book, something I need to remember to pack for a trip, or an item I want to purchase – I pull out my tiny notebook, write down a note, then go back to what I was doing. I don't have to touch my phone, and I won't see distracting notifications. So, I won't get sidetracked.

In a cascade, water collects in one pool until it overflows into the next pool. Once I have an idea in this main inbox, I can be confident I will take care of that idea, because I regularly review that inbox, moving the idea to the next appropriate inbox.

When I review my main inbox, I don't necessarily "do" the item. Usually, I simply push it further down the cascade. For example, I might write in my pocket notebook an idea for improving the Sloppy Operating Procedure for my podcast. When I review my notebook, in the Prioritize mental state, I transfer that idea to my Sloppy Operating Procedure document. Since my SOP document is sloppy, it's essentially an inbox – it can capture undeveloped ideas. I write the note at the top of the document, and I know the next time I produce podcast episodes, I'll see the idea. I can try incorporating it into my process this time around.

The "@thisweek" note I process during my weekly review is another inbox. I also have inboxes for every project I work on. I don't always capture ideas in my tiny notebook. I capture them in whichever inbox in the cascade is both appropriate and immediately accessible at the time of capture. If I have an idea for one of my projects, and I'm already on my computer, I'll quickly open up the inbox for the project that idea is for, and add to it. I also have inboxes strewn about my house. I capture ideas on small whiteboards, or even in the shower, on a waterproof notepad. Then I push the ideas further down the cascade when I get a chance.

This way, I can always quickly close the conscious loop of an idea. I can get that idea into a place where I can further engage with it later – when I'll give myself the Minimum Creative Dose, and open some subconscious loops.

FOR THE Creative Cascade to work – for it to close your conscious loops, while allowing you to open subconscious loops – you need to be able to trust you will attend to all the inboxes, so you'll get a chance to move each of your ideas further down the cascade. To keep the Creative Cascade working, you need what I call Task Triggers.

TASK TRIGGERS

A "trigger" is a stimulus that elicits a response. So, a Task Trigger is a stimulus that reminds you to do a task. To use Task Triggers effectively, strategically place your triggers. By planting Task Triggers within tasks you already know you'll do, you can make sure you do tasks you might otherwise forget.

Without knowing it, I was using Task Triggers when I was in middle school. I remember being surprised that some kids would forget to bring the right books to school, or even forget their backpacks entirely.

I never forgot my backpack, because I set it next to the doorway. I had to leave through that doorway in order to get to school, so I would have to walk past my backpack in order to do so. If I was going to be the next person to leave the house, I would even block the doorway with my backpack.

I rarely forgot to bring the right books to school because I used Task Triggers to remind me to put the right books in my bag. Each night, after brushing my teeth, part of my routine was to review what books I would need the next day, and put the right books in my bag.

I forgot my lunch most often of all, but it was still rare. I couldn't put my lunch in my bag the night before – it would spoil. Instead, I needed to remember to put my lunch in my bag after brushing my teeth in the morning.

WHY DO some Task Triggers work better than others? Because the ideal Task Trigger needs to have specific characteristics. The ideal Task Trigger is reliable, context-specific, easy-to-implement, and attached to the action.

A Task Trigger needs to be reliable, because you need to be able to count on the trigger happening. Otherwise, you can't have your mind free to focus on other things.

It needs to be context-specific because it should remind you at the exact time and place in which you can take the right action – no sooner and no later, and never in the wrong physical context. This is what's annoying about software-update notifications. Any thinking human knows that just when you're answering a call is the wrong context in which to decide to update your smartphone's operating system. The context is wrong.

A Task Trigger also needs to be easy-to-implement, because otherwise you won't be able to consistently muster the energy to follow the trigger reliably.

Finally, a good Task Trigger should be attached to the desired action itself. When the trigger happens, you don't have to do much to retrieve the object on which you'll perform the task.

I never forgot to bring my backpack to school, because my Task Trigger for bringing my backpack checked all these boxes. It was reliable, because I had no choice but to walk past my backpack on my way to school. It was context-specific, because the moment when I walked past my backpack – the stimulus – was the moment in which I needed to pick it up – the response. It was also easy to implement, because all I had to do was place my backpack by the door. Finally, it was attached to the action. The source of my trigger – my backpack – was the very object with which I needed to take action.

You can rarely construct a Task Trigger as perfect as my backpack-by-the-door trigger. In most cases, there are some trade-offs to make amongst various factors. One of those factors is that of mental load.

For example, even my backpack trigger required a small amount of mental load to follow. I had to see my backpack, and I had to remember to pick it up. This was especially true if my backpack wasn't blocking the doorway.

Remembering my lunch required the most mental load of all – which explains why it was the thing I forgot most. I had to remember to go from the bathroom to the kitchen, and open the fridge, where I'd find the lunch I had made the night before. Carrying this out of course relied upon my having made my lunch, too. This was all a lot to handle for a thirteen-year-old brain!

But mental load had to be balanced with complexity. These days, I could have my smartphone remind me a few minutes before I leave for school, either through an alarm, or a notification.

At the time, I didn't have a smartphone – they didn't exist! I suppose I could have had a giant programmable watch with a bunch of alarms, but that would have been too complex (and it probably would have made me the laughing stock of the school). So, brushing my teeth became the stimulus that triggered the response of retrieving my lunch. One habit triggered another. *Atomic Habits* author James Clear calls it "habit stacking," based upon behavioral scientist BJ Fogg's concept of "anchoring." This was such a simple solution it was worth the risk of occasionally forgetting my lunch.

Besides mental load and complexity, another factor to consider when building Task Triggers is that of distraction risk. Each time I walked from the bathroom to the kitchen to grab my lunch, I risked succumbing to the "Doorway Effect." The Doorway Effect is our tendency to forget things when we walk through a doorway. (Yes, this is an actual thing!) Additionally, I had to open the fridge, which triggers another Doorway Effect. We've all opened a fridge, only to forget why, and ended up staring at its contents for several minutes.

Distraction risk is dangerously high when you're using a smartphone for a Task Trigger. If you have to attend to something on the screen, you run the risk of seeing a distracting notification. Even touching the phone is a distraction risk for many of us – myself included.

The Creative Cascade of inboxes is run by Task Triggers. But the Creative Cascade itself also helps Task Triggers run smoothly. One Task Trigger I have is the one that gets me to write down a note in my notebook. The trigger is me thinking about something. The task is writing it down in the notebook. Then I am able to process what's in the notebook, thanks to other triggers. One such trigger is the weekly review I talked about previously. The weekly review itself is triggered by Sunday afternoons. You may remember that in my list of tasks for each weekly review is to "review inboxes." One of those inboxes is my pocket notebook.

I generally follow *Getting Things Done* rules for the items in my pocket notebook: If something on the list is going to take me two minutes or less, I do it. With longer tasks, I set something up in my task management system. But when the item on the list is an idea, rather than a task, I simply move it to the next inbox on the Creative Cascade.

Here are some items I processed from my pocket notebook during a recent weekly review:

Christmas was coming, and I had a couple different gift ideas written in my notebook. I transferred each of those items to my "gifts" inbox. I then knew that when the task of researching gifts was triggered, I would have source materials to do that research.

There were a number of things I wanted to look up on the internet. I didn't want to stop what I was doing and get off-track in order to do so, so I wrote those items in my pocket notebook. This way I could batch searches during my weekly review. I quickly did a couple searches for these items.

Also in my notebook was a book title. I have a note in which I try to categorize different types of book titles – I write books, after all! I transferred that book title into the proper category on my "book titles" note – which is essentially an inbox. There's no task assigned to this book title. My note is simply a record of my thoughts.

I also have a note in which I keep popular sayings and idioms, and try to categorize them. (The idea is that I can analyze these sayings to improve my own writing.) I had a couple popular sayings I had written in my notebook. I then transferred those sayings to this note. Again, I don't have a task assigned. This note is a place to record my thoughts, rather than ruminate about them in my head.

Finally, there were a couple interesting quotes I thought might make good source material for this book. I had come across these quotes while listening to podcasts. I wrote in my notebook quick summaries, along with which shows I heard them on, and the approximate timestamps. I then transferred those notes to my research notes in this book's project file. I wasn't yet sure whether I would use these quotes, but I knew that if I decided to use them, that would trigger me to re-listen to that portion of the podcast, to capture the exact quote.

Can you see how recording these thoughts in my pocket notebook reduced complexity and distraction risk? The notebook was quickly at hand and didn't have distracting notifications. Can you see how the triggers attached to recording, processing, and implementing these tasks helped me process everything coming my way? I was able to capture the thoughts I had, and – through regular routines such as the weekly review – send them down the Creative Cascade.

WHEN I first started writing down every idea that came to me, I found it stressful. It made me anxious because I felt I then had to do something with those ideas. It seemed I'd be better off trying to ignore these thoughts.

But I came to realize that the source of this anxiety was my mindset. By writing down ideas, I instinctively felt obligated to do something about them. That feeling of obligation then interfered with my ability to focus on the things I actually intended to do.

Once I gave myself permission to record ideas, without feeling any obligation to do anything with those ideas, capturing random ideas became incredibly productive. I freed up the conscious mental energy I was wasting on these open loops by writing them down. Yet, by writing them down, I also created subconscious open loops that allowed those ideas to incubate.

Returning to the concept of front-burner and back-burner creative energy, we can add yet another metaphor that helps us understand the power of capturing ideas, even when we don't know what we'll do with them.

The stove in my apartment in Medellín is primarily a gas stove. But way on the back left-hand side of the stove is a different unit. It's one spot on the range that isn't gas, but is instead electric. An electric burner gives you a little more control over the heat than a gas burner. In particular, it allows you to maintain a low heat for a long time. It allows you to "simmer."

CREATIVE SIMMER

Remember, front-burner projects command your best creative energy. Back-burner projects, you can complete with minimal creative energy, thanks to reliable Creative Systems.

But simmer projects are cooking almost completely in the background. Yes, once in a while you open the pot and take a peek at a simmer project. Maybe you stir it up, to keep yourself moving. But really, you could probably leave the house for days on end and that pot of vegetable stock would be delicious.

THE PLACE where the cooking metaphor starts to fall apart is that simmer projects don't need to be completed at all. Maybe your simmer projects become something someday, maybe they don't. In the meantime, you have your source materials stored somewhere you can find them. You also have open loops running in your subconscious. If the right creative opportunity comes along, you'll be ready. Instead of having a tower filled with water, it's as if the tower is filled with a complex mole sauce that has been simmering for years.

In his class on *Masterclass*, Malcolm Gladwell shared a time he traveled to a town to investigate a story. He was fascinated by what he learned there, but he soon realized his story was a dud. It wasn't until much later, when he was working on his book, *Outliers*, that he remembered that research trip. He still had recordings of his interviews, so he finally did end up using that research – or I guess it was "exploration." It took fifteen years of simmering before what he had learned became useful, but it just as easily could have never happened.

I personally keep my simmer projects in folders labeled "R&D." Companies have Research and Development departments, which expend resources on projects that may become something, or that may not become something. Amazon is famous for spending all their would-be profits on Research and Development.

Before I had my own personal R&D department, I would beat myself up for not following through on all the ideas I had. Every time I went into my files to begin working on a project, I would see countless folders of other projects that never became anything. I'd say to myself, *What's the use? I'll just abandon this project, like all of the others.*

Now, I give myself permission to keep projects in R&D until I'm sure I want to pursue them further. Not only does it keep me organized, it also keeps me sane. I'm not wasting energy feeling bad about the ideas that never become anything. They're all a part of the process. If I get a new idea for one of my R&D projects, I make sure to record it – then I let it simmer indefinitely.

THROUGHOUT THE crisis with my mother's health, I kept collecting thoughts and events in an inbox. During this period, I turned my one-hundred word AlphaSmart habit into a habit of filling this inbox. I wrote stream of consciousness into a file on the word processor, and kept adding to it every day. Later, I transferred it to my database of notes.

NOTHING HAPPENS FOR A REASON, BUT IT DOES HAPPEN

This is the part of the story where I'm supposed to tell you a miracle happened. That my mom opened her eyes, sprang up, and began to talk. Life is told in stories. Stories are better with happy endings. But happy endings don't always happen in life.

Some people say that "everything happens for a reason." I think the appropriate response to that statement is to punch the person who said it in the face. That way, when they ask why you punched them in the face for no reason, you can remind them: "Everything happens for a reason."

There's nothing good about losing someone you love. Though, my mother's death did bring new meaning to the six weeks I spent with her because of the visa and bedbug shitshow of the previous year.

Everything we experience in life is an opportunity to learn something, to make meaning out of it, and to maybe teach someone else what we learned along the way. It's the least we can do before we too part this world. With one parent gone, and my fortieth birthday not far behind me, this was top of mind as I flew back to Medellín after my emergency two-month stint in Phoenix.

I'm still processing lessons learned from the experience of losing my mother. Throughout the experience, it has been good to have a place to write those things. If not so that I can use them in some future creative work, at least to help me cope with the loss.

Throughout the tragedy of losing my mother, I was still able to keep my podcast and email newsletter coming every week. Again, when your mother is dying, who cares about your podcast and newsletter – but it was comforting to keep at least one important part of my world intact. It was possible because of my Creative Systems, and using what back-burner energy I had to do the tasks that matched my mental state.

I also kept up my habit of writing 250 words a day for this book. For such a small quantity of words, it was a surprisingly effective habit. At a pace of 250 words a day, it takes 200 days to write a 50,000-word book. If you're only writing on weekdays, that's an entire year.

On previous drafts of this book, I had aimed for a much longer daily word count. I realize now that I aimed to write more words mostly because I was terrified. I was terrified I would die before I finished. I was terrified that if I couldn't finish, I wasn't really a writer. I was terrified I was fooling myself into thinking I was ever going to finish.

But you can't rush creative work. Writing a smaller quantity of words each day left some extra energy for my Passive Genius to work with. It made my day-to-day life more enjoyable, which increased the quality of my writing. One thing I've learned having my systems put to the test is that good systems don't just take away slack – more than anything, good systems create slack. The more complex and tightly-integrated your systems, the harder they fall when one thing goes wrong. Systems should free up creative fuel, not dry up every last drop.

On my first day back in Medellín, I made a change to my morning routine. I still wrote a hundred words on my AlphaSmart. I still meditated. But I didn't then face a blank wall and work on this book. Instead, I took a shower, made myself look presentable, and stepped outside. I reacquainted myself with the sensation of outdoor air that didn't feel like it would peel the skin off my arms – in fact, the air felt like it was made for living in.

I strolled down the hill to a cafe. I put my tea on my table, set up my "grippy" tablet and keyboard combo, and looked around. There was something novel about the angle of the sun – the way it highlighted the terracotta towers rising up from the green mountain sides. There was something novel about the Colombians eating breakfast pastries and chatting at the cafe – getting off the bus dressed in their work clothes and walking to their offices with a sense of purpose in their steps.

I realized that, after four years here – four years of trying to capture that elusive, effortless creative output – this was my first time being outside on a weekday morning. And it was a glorious morning to be alive.

I put my fingers on the keyboard with the confidence of a piano prodigy. I didn't feel scared. I could do this. As Helmholtz would say, I had "turned my problem over and over in all directions." I could see the "twists and windings" of this book "in my mind's eye." Everything about how I had managed my energy and conducted my schedule had served as Preparation for this moment.

I wrote 250 words. It took fifteen minutes. I then got on with the rest of my day.

EPILOGUE

IN MY blog's income report at the beginning of 2020, I said, "I really just hope for a year without some major catastrophe." After a year of visa troubles, followed by the sudden death of my mother and helping my father get back on his feet, I was ready for life to get back to "normal" again. "But," I added, "I know this is life, and I don't have control over that."

As *my* world started to settle down, *the* world got more chaotic than it had been in a long time. As I write this, we're on what looks like the tail end of the coronavirus pandemic. I hope that if you're reading this well after 2020, that pandemic is just another event in history.

Being quarantined for months has been difficult for me, but it's been much easier than the events in my life over the previous two years. I know that hasn't been the case for millions of others whose lives and work have been directly or indirectly affected by the virus.

The onset of the coronavirus pandemic coincided with several of my multi-year projects coming to a head at once. I had just secured my first unfurnished apartment in Colombia – it was no small feat to find a landlord who would trust a foreigner. I had just moved in with my partner. I was just finishing the final chapters of this book. This life and work I had built over many years happened to be the ideal life and work for surviving the coronavirus pandemic (though my fingers are still crossed).

With many people working from home for the first time – getting everything delivered as if they were "brains in jars on Mars" – many people were also, for the first time, gaining control over how they used their time. Aside from the emotional concerns of trying to focus on work while the world was in crisis, people were also grappling with how to prioritize, stay motivated, and think clearly while working from home, when the clock wasn't dictating their every move. Suddenly they had the time, but they needed to find the energy.

TO START managing your creative energy, start by rethinking time. Be on the lookout for time worship. Time usually isn't what you're optimizing for. Work according to clock-time only when it really matters. Otherwise, work according to event-time. Don't try to cram certain outcomes into units of time. Instead, use units of time as rough guides to allocate your energy into activities that will move you toward your goals.

Find your Creative Sweet Spot. Find one block of time each day that you can clear away, and spend that time in the Generate mental state. You're probably most creative first thing in the morning, so experiment with the First Hour Rule. Remember, your Creative Sweet Spot is not the time when your mind is sharpest. You want to think divergently so you can have insights. Later on, you can think convergently and turn those ideas into finished products.

When a creative problem gets tough, remember to respect the Four Stages of Creativity. If you're struggling to find a moment of Illumination, you probably need more Preparation and Incubation. Don't expect your work to be ready to ship the moment you have a great idea. You have to do Verification to find out if ideas that are novel are also useful.

Notice the mental states in your work. Remember: PERGPAR – PER Golf, PAR. Prioritize, Explore, Research, Generate, Polish, Administrate, and Recharge. It takes practice to recognize what mental states best fit the various parts of your work. Build mastery in one mental state at a time. Start by separating out Generate work. Then make Prioritization a priority. Let the other mental states fall into place around those "big rocks." You'll notice some fuzzy borders amongst these states, so be flexible. Be mindful of the tools you use and the settings in which you do your work. How do your tools and environment affect your mental state? Choose grippy tools when your ideas are starting to develop, and choose slippy tools when you're ready to execute.

Start searching for Creative Cycles in your work, and in the rhythms of the world around you. The better you can break your work into repeatable projects, the better you'll become at recognizing Creative Cycles and harnessing their power. Start building a weekly routine, and notice the patterns you see throughout longer cycles, such as a typical month or a typical year.

As you master Creative Cycles, you can start building Creative Systems. Create Sloppy Operating Procedure documents, and build upon them as you go. Experiment with what compromises you can make in your creative projects. Can you create constraints that make your system repeatable without reducing the quality of your ideas? As you establish your systems, you can produce consistently with your back-burner energy, thus freeing up front-burner energy to work on one-off projects, or build additional systems.

Finally, build systems that not only withstand the chaos of life, but that improve from that chaos. You can't build systems that depend upon everything going perfectly, because chaos is life's only constant. When chaos does strike, be ready with a Creative Cascade of inboxes. Capture Creative Opportunities as they come, and store them where you can develop them later. Build a series of Task Triggers, so you can be confident you'll engage with your ideas when needed. Try to make your Task Triggers reliable, context-specific, easy-to-implement, and attached to the action. After enough practice with the Seven Mental States, you should be ready to organize your tasks not by project, but by mental state.

ASIDE FROM the time I was changing my clothes in a filthy laundromat bathroom in Chicago, there are other times when I ask myself, "How the hell did I end up here?" In fact, I ask myself that nearly every day.

Steven Pressfield wrote in one of his books that a friend told him you can never plan your life. Too many unexpected things happen. His friend said, "You meet someone and you wind up living in another country, speaking a different language." That sums up my life at this point: I write English to the world in the day, and speak Spanish to my life partner in the night. My little experiment turned into a permanent life change. Whether I'm grinding freshly-picked *chócolo* to make *arepas* in the Colombian countryside, watching a pair of giant scarlet Macaws fly over my building in Medellín, or simply waking up in the morning and watching the clouds burn off the surrounding mountains, I'm frequently awestruck at where I've ended up.

When I began this journey in this foreign country, I wanted all my possessions to fit into three suitcases. I'm way beyond that point now. I not only have the desk I slid into the white-walled cove, but I have an office chair to go with it. I have my own bookcase and bed and dining table, a large L-shaped couch and a growing collection of plants. I no longer pay one lump sum to a vacation rental company. Ironically, I'm not yet established enough as a Colombian resident to have my rent and electric bill and internet bill on auto-pay. I have to pay them manually, and, as if I were a caveman, I sometimes even have to walk into a bank.

When I first embarked on this adventure, I figured I would eventually return to normal life. It turned out that normal life is happening right here in Colombia. Fortunately, I have the contents of this book to help me fill that life with creative work. I hope this book also helps you to manage this seismic shift in life and work.

ACKNOWLEDGEMENTS

THANK YOU to the following readers, who provided early feedback on this book.

Cyndi Casey
Wez Coffey
Tony Crockford
Helena Denley
Cheryl Hulseapple
June Gilbank
Masumi Goldman
Elizabeth Kuehn

Cornelis van Lit
Andrew Miller
Cary Millsap
Devon Ostendorf
Eric Renn
Ed Stanfield
Kate Stanton

THANK YOU to the following readers, who purchased the Preview Edition of this book:

Clyde Adams III
Andy Angelos
Susan B.
Jordan Baker
William Bartholomew
Akshay Bhalotia
Suzanne Bird-Harris
MV Braverman
Andrew Broman
Jakob Bruhns
Ian Cameron
Cyndi Casey

Beto Caceres Castro
Annie Cheney
Wez Coffey
Sean Corbett
Tim Courtney
Bobby Craig
Tony Crockford
Jakub Danielka
Matthew W Darlison
Brandon Dauphinais
Helena Denley
Emre Deveci

Erik Didriksen

Thinh Dinh

Kathleen Donohue

Jason Douglas

Олег Ефимов

Richard F. Emerson

Jill Fechner

Thorvald Finnbjornsson

Jacob G.

Masumi Goldman

Peggy Grant

Chantelle Griffiths

Christopher Hagad

Daren Heidgerken

Fern Horst

David Ryan Huff

Mary DeRosa Hughes

Uwe Husmann

Soley J

Ario Jafarzadeh

JM&TB

Ritu Kaushal

David Ker

Matt Lacey

Ian Lawton

Adrian Lee

Liz. "Older 81 yr. lady, not old"

Sam Lopes

Amanda Maintenance

Brian McCann

Paul McGlinchey

Matthew McMillion

Alice Merry

Andy Miller

John Mitchell

Ian Molee

Nanci Murdock

Brennon Murphy

Michael Nazari

L. Amber O'Hearn

Sean Oliver

Tim Oslovich

Raúl Palacios

Jeffrey T. Palmer

Sumit Parab

Keith R. Parsons

Ajith Peter

Daniel Porter

Paolo-R

Umesh Rao

George V. Reilly

Alejandro Renteria

Tom Rivers

Craig Scott Roberts

Christopher Roby

Roders

Carlos Rodriguez

Jeremie Rykner

Kevin Sampson

Ramin Saraby

Francisco Saravia

Dhairya Hemendra
Alpa Shah

Roza Robot Shershnyaga

Dr. Eliezer Shore

Sjoerd Siebinga

K. Sisti

Bardees Smairat

Braden Smith

Ed Stanfield

Kate Stanton

Gladys Strickland

Ariel Strong

Melissa and Tawny

Rev. Lucas Thompson

Milo Todorovich

Aimee Tweedie

Michael Urbonas

Alfonso Urzua

Masood Ahmed Usmani

Cornelis van Lit

Charlotte Vera

Nicky Waites

Michael Whitmore

Mark Wiseman

Thai Wood

Wang Yip

Matt Zehner

NOTES

CHAPTER 1

Kai-Fu Lee talks about optimization-based jobs with narrow tasks vs. jobs requiring creativity in an unstructured environment in his book *AI Superpowers: China, Silicon Valley, and the New World Order*.

Janelle Shane's tweet about AI writing is at https://twitter.com/JanelleCShane/status/1196827079599255552

Frederick Taylor described his process of developing processes for moving "pig iron" in his book, *The Principles of Scientific Management*.

Mark Manson talks about having a "God value" in his book, *Everything is F*cked: A Book About Hope*.

Harold Pashler found that people have very little capacity to multitask in "Dual-task interference in simple tasks: Data and theory," Psychological Bulletin, Vol 116(2), Sep 1994, 220–244.

The CDC reports that 30% of working Americans get less than six hours of sleep: https://www.cdc.gov/niosh/topics/repro/workschedule.html (accessed August 2020) The CDC recommends anywhere from 7–9 hours of sleep for adults, depending upon age: https://www.cdc.gov/sleep/about_sleep/how_much_sleep.html (accessed August 2020)

The deleterious effects of a lack of sleep are sourced from the book *Why We Sleep: Unlocking the Power of Sleep and Dreams*, by Matthew Walker.

The direct effects of caffeine are hard to study in human subjects, since caffeine is so prevalent that it's hard to separate its positive effects from merely reducing withdrawal. (Rogers and Dernoncourt 1998) Hameleers et al. did see a slight improvement in delayed recall with caffeine, but that was only after a twenty-minute delay; (2000) Herz found no effect on memory with a two-day delay (1999); and Borota et al. (2014) found caffeine to improve retention if administered after – but not before – being presented with information. On the contrary, Mednick et al. found napping to be better at memory formation than caffeine (2008). However, what I'm talking about when I mention a "downward spiral" is the long-term effects that copious amounts of caffeine is likely to have on memory consolidation over the long term. Sleep is critical to memory consolidation (Stickgold 2005) and caffeine disrupts sleep (Landolt 1995).

Jason Fried talks about "calendar Tetris" in his book, *It Doesn't Have to Be Crazy at Work.*

I first heard of Bill Gates's "Think Week," and how it led to writing a memo about building a web browser, from *Deep Work: Rules for Focused Success in a Distracted World.*

Stephen King recommends novelists to put their first draft in a drawer for six weeks, before reviewing it, in his book, *On Writing: A Memoir of the Craft.*

Mason Currey's *Daily Rituals: Women at Work* says Elizabeth Bishop took twenty years between starting and finishing her poem, "The Moose."

Malcolm Gladwell says "the first task of a writer is to create enough space and time for writing to emerge," in his interview on Neil Pasricha's *3 Books* podcast.

Joseph Heller's quote about daydreaming is from *Daily Rituals: How Artists Work.*

George Carlin recommends daydreaming in his stand-up special, *You Are All Diseased.* The track on the album is called "Kids and Parents."

The anecdote about the sculptor Marisol sitting so still spiders built webs on her, the quote from Alice Walker about inviting creativity, and the quote from Marian Anderson about useless labor suddenly bearing fruit, are all from *Mason Currey's Daily Rituals: Women at Work.*

I first saw the quote from Constantin Brancusi about being in the right state of mind to make things in *Daily Rituals: Women at Work.* Maggi Hambling paraphrased the quote. I don't know when Brancusi originally said this.

I can't find any proof that Maya Angelou ever said anything about the agony of bearing an untold story. Goodreads says it's from *I Know Why the Caged Bird Sings,* but it's not. It's quoted in books, on merchandise – it's everywhere. It rings true, and seems like something she would write, so I had to use it.

Viktor Frankl talks about bearing any "how" once you know the "why" of your existence in *Man's Search for Meaning.* It's a paraphrase from Friedrich Nietzsche, from the book, *Twilight of the Idols, or, How to Philosophize with a Hammer.*

Daniel Pink talks about the practice of sending adolescents to school outside of their biological rhythms in his book *When: The Scientific Secrets of Perfect Timing.*

CHAPTER 2

Maya Angelou talks about her practice of renting a hotel room near her house in an interview in issue 116 of the *Paris Review*. I sourced it from a collection of such interviews, a book called *The Paris Review Interviews, IV*. It's also available for paid subscribers here: https://www.theparisreview.org/interviews/2279/maya-angelou-the-art-of-fiction-no-119-maya-angelou I first read about it in *Daily Rituals: How Artists Work.*

Divergent and convergent thinking originated with psychologist J. P. Guilford's "structure of intellect" theory, published in the Psychological Bulletin, 53(4), 267–293, in 1956.

John Konious defined insight to me in our conversation on my podcast, *Love Your Work*, episode 8 https://kadavy.net/blog/posts/love-your-work-episode-8-creating-aha-moments-with-neuroscientist-dr-john-kounios/

Leon Kreitzman describes the circadian "drive" and the "homeostatic" drive in his book, *The Rhythms of Life: The Biologic Drives that Control the Daily Lives of Every Living Thing*. For simplicity's sake, I call the homeostatic drive the "sleep debt" system, which is how it was described in *Why We Sleep: Unlocking the Power of Sleep and Dreams*, by Matthew Walker.

For siesta habits across cultures, see W. B. Webb et al.'s "Cultural perspectives on napping and the siesta." In *Sleep and Alertness: Chronobiological, Behavioral, and Medical Aspects of Napping* 1989; pp. 247–266.

Times during which creators worked are from either *Daily Rituals: How Artists Work*, or *Daily Rituals: Women at Work*, both by Mason Curry. The exception is Tim Ferriss, who has mentioned his preference for nighttime writing in more podcast conversations than I could count.

Reverberi et al. (2005) showed that patients with prefrontal cortex damage were almost twice as likely as normal patients to solve a difficult insight problem, in their study, "Better without (lateral) frontal cortex? Insight problems solved by frontal patients" *Brain*, Volume 128, Issue 12, Pages 2882–2890. I first read about this study in John Kounios and Mark Beeman's *The Eureka Factor: Aha Moments, Creative Insight, and the Brain.*

For simplicity's sake, I'm conflating grogginess with your off-peak time of day. So if you're an evening person, you're most creative in the morning. If you're a morning person, you're most creative in the evening. Neuroscientists John Kounios and Mark Beeman write in their book *The Eureka Factor: Aha Moments, Creative Insight, and the Brain*, "For creativity, your finest hour is literally the low point of your day."

John Kounios and Mark Beeman's quote about doing idea generation while sleep deprived is from a conversation I had with him over email.

Robert Levine talks about the difference between "clock-time" and "event-time" cultures in his book, *A Geography of Time: The Temporal Misadventures of a Social Psychologist.*

Paul McCarney shared the story of a chauffeur inspiring "Eight Days a Week" in *The Beatles Anthology*, 2000.

Tamar Avnet and Anne-Laure Sellier found that both clock-time and event-time approaches can lead to good outcomes in their paper, "Clock time vs. event time: Temporal culture or self-regulation?" *Journal of Experimental Social Psychology*, Volume 47, Issue 3, May 2011, Pages 665–667.

Teresa M. Amabile et al. studied time pressure's effect on creativity in their working paper, "Time Pressure And Creativity In Organizations: A Longitudinal Field Study," 2002.

The sexagesimal system, with which we measure time, was adopted by the Babylonians from the Sumerians. However, the Babylonians also created the 360-degree circle, on which our sixty seconds and minutes are arranged: https://www.nytimes.com/2013/07/09/science/60-behind-every-second-millenniums-of-history.html (accessed August 2020)

Though other inaccurate attempts were made previously, Jost Burgi created the first known mechanical clock that accurately kept time to the minute in the late sixteenth century. From the *Biographical Dictionary of the History of Technology*, by Lance Day and Ian MacNeil.

Christian Huygens produced the first clock that accurately counted seconds in 1657. https://ieee-uffc.org/about-us/history/uffc-s-history/the-evolution-of-the-quartz-crystal-clock/ (accessed August 2020)

Essen and Parry reported that the caesium-133 atom could keep accurate time in their 1955 paper, "An Atomic Standard of Frequency and Time Interval: A Cæsium Resonator," *Nature*, Volume 176, Issue 4476, pp. 280–282.

I first heard of Dean Simonton's work on creative output and quality from Adam Grant's *Originals: How Non-Conformists Move the World*. The output numbers of Picasso and Beethoven are sourced from *Originals*.

The Georgia O'Keeffe Museum reports that she painted approximately 2,000 paintings here: https://www.okeeffemuseum.org/store/products/books-media/georgia-okeeffe/okeeffes-okeeffes-the-artists-collection/ (accessed August 2020)

CHAPTER 3

Helmholtz's speech was originally in German, and I've seen it translated in English in a number of places, with slightly differing translations. Still, the general spirit of the speech is always the same. I got my translation from the earliest source I could find: in the book, *Hermann Von Helmholtz*, by Leo Königsberger, translated by Frances Alice Welby, 1906. Page 209. I first read about the speech in John Kounios and Mark Beeman's *The Eureka Factor*.

Graham Wallas expands on Helmholtz's speech, describing the "stages of control," in his book, *The Art of Thought*. I first heard about this book from John Kounios and Mark Beeman's *The Eureka Factor*.

Mason Currey's *Daily Rituals: Women at Work* says Elizabeth Bishop took twenty years between starting and finishing her poem, "The Moose."

Michelangelo's method of gradually lifting a scale model out of a basin of water while carving is described in Vasari's *Lives of the Artists: Biographies of the Most Eminent Architects, Painters, and Sculptors of Italy*, edited by Betty Burroughs, Simon and Schuster, 1946, page 293. I found this source through http://www.michelangelomodels.com/m-models/how-he-made/water_model_vasari.html

Ross King talks about Michelangelo crafting his image as "the divine one" in *Michelangelo and The Pope's Ceiling*.

In case you recognized it, yes, the idea of feeling like a mouse drowning in cream is inspired by the movie, *Catch Me if You Can*.

The story of how Paul McCartney composed "Yesterday" comes from a mixture of sources. There's an entire book about it, Ray Coleman's *McCartney: Yesterday and Today*. His quote about going around for weeks playing the chords for people is from the December 1984 issue of *Playboy* magazine.

You may have noticed that the lyrics of "Yesterday" don't include the words "merrily" or "funnily." But, that was part of his process, as quoted on page 204 of Barry Miles's *Paul McCartney: Many Years From Now*.

My description of relational memory is adapted for simplicity from "Human relational memory requires time and sleep," by Ellenbogen et al., *Proceedings of the National Academy of Sciences of the USA* 104 (2007): 7723–28. I first read about it in John Kounios and Mark Beeman's *The Eureka Factor: Aha Moments, Creative Insight, and the Brain*.

Meredith Monk's practice of drawing charts and maps to understand elements of a piece is from *Daily Rituals: Women at Work*.

There are studies suggesting that the unconscious mind does actively work on creative problems during Incubation. However, I defer to neuroscientist John Kounios on this, who has told me these studies aren't conclusive and the jury is still out.

Maya Angelou's quote about putting her writing out of her mind in the evenings is sourced from *Daily Rituals: How Artists Work*.

Stephen King recommends novelists to put their first draft in a drawer for six weeks, before reviewing it, in his book, *On Writing: A Memoir of the Craft*.

Lillian Hellman's writing process is described in *Daily Rituals: Women at Work*.

CHAPTER 4

Quotes from Cal Newport are from my conversation with him on my podcast, *Love Your Work*, episode 183: https://kadavy.net/blog/posts/cal-newport-podcast-interview/

The "Scrambled Eggs" placeholder lyrics for "Yesterday" are from Ray Coleman's *McCartney: Yesterday and Today*. For fun, search around on the internet and see if you can find the video of McCartney performing the song with these placeholder lyrics – as well as some new embellishments – on *Tonight Show Starring Jimmy Fallon*.

For more on L-Theanine's synergistic relationship with caffeine, see "The effects of l-theanine, caffeine and their combination on cognition and mood", by Haskell et al. *Biological Psychology*, Volume 77, Issue 2, February 2008, Pages 113–122. Consult your doctor before taking any supplements.

Van Gogh focusing on black and white before moving on to color is described in *Van Gogh: A Life*, by Steven Naifeh.

Georgia O'Keeffe focused on black and white drawing after leaving art school in New York, as discussed in the anthology of her correspondence with her friend, Anna Pollitzer, *Lovingly, Georgia*.

Quotes of Donald M. Rattner are from my conversation with him on my podcast, *Love Your Work*, episode 201: https://kadavy.net/blog/posts/donald-m-rattner/

The study showing stock traders on higher floors taking bigger risks is "The Influence of Physical Elevation in Buildings on Risk Preferences: Evidence from a Pilot and Four Field Studies," by Esteky et al., *Journal of*

Consumer Psychology, Volume 28, Issue 3, July 2018, Pages 487–494. I first heard of it from my podcast conversation with Donald M. Rattner, cited above.

The study showing the optimal noise level for creativity at around seventy decibels is "Is Noise Always Bad? Exploring the Effects of Ambient Noise on Creative Cognition," by Mehta et al., *Journal of Consumer Research*, Volume 39, Issue 4, 1 December 2012, Pages 784–799. I first read about it in Donald M. Rattner's *My Creative Space*, and was reminded of it in my podcast conversation with him, cited above.

Creators who created in bed or reclining are from multiple sources. I read about Marcel Proust, Michael Chabon, and Truman Capote in Donald M. Rattner's *My Creative Space*. I read about René Descartes in *Daily Rituals: How Artists Work*. I read about Edith Wharton and Frida Kahlo in *Daily Rituals: Women at Work*.

Twyla Tharp's cab-hailing habit is from *The Creative Habit: Learn it and Use it for Life*.

Mark McGuinness describes how his Japanese *Star Wars* mug puts him in the right mental state for writing in my conversation with him on my podcast, *Love Your Work*, episode 163: https://kadavy.net/blog/posts/mark-mcguinness-podcast/

Nicholson Baker's "placebo effect" quote is from *Daily Rituals: How Artists Work*.

CHAPTER 5

Ari Meisel's quotes are from his Udemy course, *The Art of Less Doing*, which is no longer available.

I first read about the planning fallacy in Daniel Kahneman's *Thinking, Fast and Slow*.

I learned about the prefrontal cortex being particularly energy-hungry from David Rock's *Your Brain at Work: Strategies for Overcoming Distraction, Regaining Focus, and Working Smarter All Day Long*.

Steve Jobs told *Fortune* magazine he was as proud of the things Apple didn't do as the things Apple did do in March of 2008: https://archive.fortune.com/galleries/2008/fortune/0803/gallery.jobsqna.fortune/6.html (accessed August 2020)

The quotes from John Kounios about the benefits of the Week of Want are from my conversation with him on my podcast, *Love Your Work*, episode 8 https://kadavy.net/blog/posts/love-your-work-episode-8-

creating-aha-moments-with-neuroscientist-dr-john-kounios/

The quote from former Google CEO Eric Schmidt about the 20% time policy is from the *Masters of Scale* podcast. Clip here: https://www.youtube.com/watch?v=QMW8ZsXxOKw (accessed August 2020)

I first heard of Bill Gates's "Think Week," and how it led to writing a memo about building a web browser, from *Deep Work: Rules for Focused Success in a Distracted World*.

The quote from Paul Jarvis about his month-long winter break from social media is from an email conversation.

Jason Fried talks about the practice of breaking projects down to six weeks, then taking two weeks off, in his book, *It Doesn't Have to Be Crazy at Work*. The quote about fasting is from my conversation with him on my podcast, *Love Your Work*, episode 147: https://kadavy.net/blog/posts/jason-fried-podcast-2/

The study that demonstrates a wage increase due to extra sleep gained being on a different side of a time zone is *Time Use and Productivity: The Wage Returns to Sleep*, by Gibson and Shrader, 2014.

CHAPTER 6

Dr. Robert Maurer's story about asking about car colors is from my conversation with him on my podcast, *Love Your Work*, episode 187: https://kadavy.net/blog/posts/robert-maurer-kaizen/

The term "Baader-Meinhof phenomenon" – sometimes conflated with the "frequency illusion" – was coined on an internet message board in 1994. The thread is saved for posterity here: https://www.twincities.com/2012/08/15/watch-a-hummingbird-at-the-feeder-fending-off-all-other-hummers-the-rest-of-the-day/ (accessed August 2020)

The story about Charles Goodyear "accidentally" discovering the process for vulcanizing rubber is from the book *Napoleon's Buttons: How 17 Molecules Changed History*.

The story about Ira Glass from the *Longform* podcast is from episode 159: https://longform.org/posts/longform-podcast-159-ira-glass (accessed August 2020)

The study cited in *David Rock's Your Brain at Work: Strategies for Overcoming Distraction, Regaining Focus, and Working Smarter All Day Long*, which showed implicit learning of keyboard patterns was Rauch, S. L., C. R. Savage, H. D. Brown, T. Curran, N. M. Alpert, A. Kendrick, A. J. Fischman, and S. M. Kosslyn. "A PET Investigation of Implicit and

Explicit Sequence Learning." *Human Brain Mapping*, 3 (1995): 271–86.

I learned about hand-crafted cars ending up different sizes from *The Machine That Changed the World: The Story of Lean Production – Toyota's Secret Weapon in the Global Car Wars That Is Now Revolutionizing World Industry*, by James P. Womack, Daniel T. Jones, and Daniel Roos.

The "All is Lost" moment is a popular screenwriting device, which originated in Blake Snyder's *Save the Cat: The Last Book on Screenwriting You'll Ever Need*. I first heard of it from Stephen Pressfield's *Nobody Wants to Read Your Sh*t: Why That Is And What You Can Do About It*.

CHAPTER 7

Nassim Nicholas Taleb talks about systems that benefit from chaos in his book, *Antifragile: Things That Gain from Disorder*.

For more on grief's effects on cognitive function, see "Cognitive functioning in complicated grief," Charles A. Hall et al., *Journal of Psychiatric Research*, Volume 58, November 2014, Pages 20–25. I first heard about these effects from *It's OK That You're Not OK*, by Megan Devine. (And personal experience, of course.)

Jon Bokenkamp shared his screenwriting process with me on my podcast, *Love Your Work*, episode 93: https://kadavy.net/blog/posts/jon-bokenkamp/

Seth Godin wrote about water towers in his blog post, "Water towers": https://seths.blog/2019/12/water-towers/ (accessed August 2020)

"The Doorway Effect" was coined by psychologist Tom Stafford: https://mindhacks.com/2016/03/11/why-you-forget-what-you-came-for-when-you-enter-the-room/ (accessed August 2020)

ABOUT THE AUTHOR

DAVID KADAVY is a bestselling author whose books help people be productive when creativity matters. He was design advisor for behavioral scientist Dan Ariely's productivity app, Timeful, where David's "mind management" principles were applied to features now used by millions – in Google Calendar. He lives in Medellín, Colombia. Follow him on Twitter or Instagram at @kadavy.

This page intentionally has only this sentence.